SURRENDER TO WIN

Regain Sanity by Strategically
Relinquishing Control

Laura Harris

GREENLEAF
BOOK GROUP PRESS

Published by Greenleaf Book Group Press
4425 S. Mo Pac Expwy., Suite 600
Austin, Texas 78735

Distributed by Greenleaf Book Group LLC

For ordering information or special discounts for bulk purchases, please contact Greenleaf Book Group LLC at 4425 S. Mo Pac Expwy., Austin, TX 78735, (512) 891-6100.

Design and composition by Greenleaf Book Group LLC
Cover design by Greenleaf Book Group LLC

Publisher's Cataloging-In-Publication Data

Harris, Laura D.
  Surrender to win : regain sanity by strategically relinquishing control /
Laura Harris. -- 1st ed.

   p. ; cm.

  ISBN: 978-1-929774-55-5

1. New business enterprises--United States—Management. 2. Small business--United States—Management. 3. Small business--Finance. 4. Entrepreneurship--United States. I. Title.

HD62.5 .H27 2009
658.11   2008931120

Part of the Tree Neutral™ program that offsets the number of trees consumed in printing this book by taking proactive steps such as planting trees in direct proportion to the number of trees used. www.treeneutral.com

TreeNeutral

Printed in the United States of America on acid-free paper

08 09 10 11 12 13 14   10 9 8 7 6 5 4 3 2 1

First Edition

To my family, friends, and mentors—
God has used you to stretch me.

Contents

INTRODUCTION

O UT OF THE frying pan and into the fire. That is how I would describe the initial jump from being an employee to being self-employed. I wish I had known then what I know now. I wish I had made many decisions differently. There were flaws in my business planning and my recruiting process, in how I managed and mismanaged people. There were smart decisions and naïve ones. I asked myself, "What do I wish someone had told me that could have saved my employees and me a lot of grief?"

This book holds the answers to those hard-earned lessons. Whether you are a business owner or work in a business that you would like to run more smoothly, you'll learn how to avoid costly, time-consuming trial-and-terror learning. If you apply the concepts in this book, you can immediately begin to

- Generate more income and maximize profits;
- Build better relationships with your clients and co-workers;
- Systemize your office procedures to reduce duplicate efforts;
- Create client loyalty so customers become your ambassadors;
- Develop autonomous employees who are resourceful and self-motivated;
- Decrease the stress that results from "making it up as you go along."

My biggest mistake was creating a tremendously successful business that revolved around me. When I went on my first vacation I finally grasped how crucial it would be to design a business that worked without me—not because of me. I had to surrender control of my business in order for it to grow long term. I could only win in business if I strategically relinquished control.

This book outlines four steps to building a profitable business. The sections categorize the concepts as follows:

AUTOPILOT LEADERSHIP

Leadership skills developed throughout the organization impact the success and sustainability of a business. Leadership that revolves around the strength of the team, not the knowledge of the owner, creates long-term prosperity. Are you able to paint a clear vision of where the business is going? Do you continually commit to learning yourself and building those around you? Does your walk in life match your talk?

UPFRONT ALIGNMENT

A strong foundation allows a business to thrive and to adapt easily. Do you have a functional business plan that includes a clear marketing strategy? Have you created an employee handbook to provide clarity around job expectations? Are written goals created by the team? Are the goals of the organization and the individuals aligned? Is the productivity of the team measured on an ongoing basis and shared throughout the organization?

TEAM ON TARGET

Employees are either your biggest headache or the solution to your problems in business. An ideal business is one where the leader and the employees both feel they have the good end of the deal. I feel blessed to work with my team and it is my responsibility to design a career they would be crazy to leave. Is there a clear hiring plan? Are you sure you are hiring the best candidates? Do you have confidence in the organization's ability to attract, educate, and motivate personnel? Are employees held accountable for helping the organization reach its goals?

DEVIL'S IN THE DETAILS

Now it is time to get down to work. Is there a clearly defined direction for the day-to-day operations of the business? How will you attract and retain customers? How can you create a business with fewer monster clients? Can you and everyone within your operation clearly articulate what makes your business unique? Are clients confident that they will have a positive, consistent experience with your organization regardless of who assists them?

My fondest hope is that this book has a dramatic, immediate, and positive impact on the way you do business. By sharing my experiences and the insight gained by studying hundreds of businesses, I will assist you at work and at home in creating the quality of life you want, need, and deserve. I hope you'll enjoy these thoughts and stories. You will probably recognize yourself in many of these situations. Chances are you have already learned some of these lessons—the hard way. Keep in mind: "Knowing something does not mean you are doing it."

At the end of a chapter you may think, "That is obvious. Everyone knows that." But ask the question, *"Am I doing it?"* As one of my favorite Chinese proverbs says, "Just because something is common sense does not mean it is common practice."

We don't need dozens of diet books to teach us that there are two things needed for weight loss—eat right and exercise. Unfortunately, without the appropriate action, that knowledge is irrelevant. Information without action is useless. If you read a chapter about the importance of putting together an employee handbook, don't just nod your head in agreement and think, "That is a great idea!" Don't add it to your "to do" list. I would imagine that list is long enough already. Get on the Internet and download a sample handbook or assign the task to someone in your office—*immediately*. I encourage you to go through this book with your staff. Work together on building a better business one chapter at a time. Use this book as a catalyst to change the way you do business.

This book is divided into short chapters, which allows even the busiest individual to jump in and derive value in just a few minutes. Get out a pen or pencil and take the time to underline key passages. Write notes in the margin and on your calendar, creating an action plan as you go.

Years ago I was sitting in the back row of a Zig Ziglar seminar waiting for the program to begin. Zig walked up to the microphone and announced, "If anyone would like to have their book signed, I will be glad to sign autographs for the next fifteen minutes." I had brought along my copy of his book *Ziglar on Selling*. I was completely engrossed and highly motivated to act when I read it. I really wanted his autograph but was not interested in going on stage. I took the wimpy way out and begged a friend to get my book signed.

I watched from the back of the room while Mr. Ziglar opened my book. He looked surprised when he opened the inside cover and began flipping through the pages. At that moment I remembered I had written notes throughout the book. He looked at my friend and asked, loud enough for everyone in the room to hear, "Is this your book?"

Panic set in. I wanted to scream, "Never mind the autograph, I'm sorry." Unfortunately, escape was impossible. I was praying my friend would claim the book. Instead he pointed to me and said, "Nope, it's hers."

All eyes were instantly on me. Mr. Ziglar explained, "Now this is the way a book should be read." He held up the book, showing the scribbled-upon pages, and announced, "See the notes in the margins? She has underlined and highlighted passages. Notice that she has referenced her favorite pages on the inside front cover."

I was so glad he understood that writing all over the book was not a sign of disrespect. I was designing a personal action plan as I read through the pages. His book had touched me and changed the way I did business.

I hope you'll read this book in the same manner. These are real-life situations and solutions you can implement immediately. Reevaluate your business annually as you re-read the book and realize that your business faces different challenges as it evolves and grows. If your perspective and behavior changes after you've read the book, we will both have invested our time wisely.

Ready to get started? Grab a pen and a highlighter, turn the page, and let's grow.

Part 1

AUTOPILOT LEADERSHIP

Look Before You Leap

Research is what I'm doing when I don't know what I'm doing.
—Wernher Magnus Maximilian von Braun

I DID NOT GROW up dreaming of being self-employed. I enjoyed working for someone else. I certainly did not long for the financial risk or stress involved in jumping into business on my own. Over the years, however, I became frustrated with several work situations and began to long for the freedom that I perceived business owners experienced. I fantasized about the ability to come and go as I pleased. I also assumed that business owners earned much more money than I was accustomed to making.

When I did begin to contemplate opening a business I met with a gentleman named Mark. I trusted him to provide me with a clear direction on how to get started. I distinctly remember our initial meeting. We had lunch at a Chili's restaurant, and I even remember what I ate—Caribbean salad!

I was fairly young, thirty-three years old. I respected my current boss tremendously and loved my job. I was, however, excited about the glamour that was attached to being self-employed. And after more than a decade of working for other people in the insurance industry and a degree in Business Management, I was ready to go.

I walked into lunch thinking Mark would try to convince me that being an entrepreneur would drastically improve my life. With visions of freedom dancing in my head, I had already decided to jump. Imagine my surprise when the meeting turned out to be just the opposite of what I had envisioned! He actually tried to talk me *out* of opening a business. He pointed out every possible pitfall, shortfall, and downfall. He made it clear that I would have to work longer hours and the money would not come flowing in immediately. Reality check!!!

Mark challenged my desire to open a business. His honest approach caught me off guard. He urged me to think about whether or not I was willing to make the sacrifices necessary and take the risks required. He was concerned that I may not have a realistic perspective about how much money it would take to start a business and forced me to contemplate the negative aspects of business ownership. I respect him tremendously for painting a realistic rather than an idealistic picture.

I had naïvely thought that owning a business would be glamorous. I was excited about the ability to have rewards based on my efforts. I imagined how exciting it would be without seriously contemplating potential risks and responsibilities.

Thanks to Mark, I realized I had better do some research. I needed to make an educated decision, not an emotional one.

After my wake-up call, I spoke to several business owners and began to read voraciously. I wanted to be very aware of what it would take to succeed in business.

After examining all the possible scenarios, I decided I had done enough research to make an informed decision. I was prepared to make the sacrifices that would be necessary to achieve success. I was finally prepared enough to reduce the risk of failure. I had done my research before becoming self-employed.

THOUGHT-PROVOKING QUESTIONS AND ACTION PLANS

1. Does the thought of being your own boss sound glamorous? Do you anticipate that owning a business would resolve current frustrations? What appeals most to you about owning a business?

2. Do you truly have an entrepreneurial spirit? Do you have a desire to be the largest and the best? Do you have a high tolerance for risk? Are you willing to reinvest profits back into your business to maximize growth?

3. Before you move ahead, have several successful business owners play devil's advocate for you. Do you know a trusted individual who is successful in your industry? Set up a meeting. Ask if she/he will pose every possible catastrophe so you can consider the pros and cons. If you can be talked out of starting a business, chances are you are not ready.

4. Is your spouse or significant other enthusiastic about your being in business? Will you be able to balance the pressures of being self-employed with the other aspects of your life?

5. Stop and think about whether or not you will really enjoy being in the industry you have chosen for the next twenty years. Are you getting into the contemplated industry for the right reasons? Will this work create a sense of fulfillment?

6. We all know that most people can be quite content working for someone else. If you are considering becoming self-employed, you have effectively chosen to "lay off the boss." Was it a wise decision? How do you plan to design a business where others will enjoy working—so *you* don't get laid off?

Am I Riding the Horse or Is the Horse Riding Me?

Drive thy business or it will drive thee.
—Benjamin Franklin

O NE OF MY favorite hobbies is riding horses. It is a love my daughters and I share. On weekends we go to a local stable, rent horses, and ride on the beach.

One day I had a particularly exhilarating ride on a new horse named Comet. Suffice it to say, she was a handful. I had to keep a tight rein the entire time or she would have run away with me. My daughter Kara noticed I was grinning from ear to ear and commented, "Mom, I can tell you love that horse." I instinctively responded, "I love her because I am not sure who is in control. I'm not sure if I'm riding her or if she is riding me."

While driving home we talked about the excitement of riding on the wild side. It dawned on me that lack of control might be exhilarating with horses but not in business. I thought of my first vacation exactly one year after becoming self-employed. It should have been a relaxing time on the beaches of Cancun, Mexico. Instead, it entailed me running from the beach to the hotel five or six times a day to call the office. I could not relax. I realized there were several aspects of the business that only I was trained to handle. I had unintentionally created a business that revolved around me. I definitely was not riding this horse—it was riding me. I was completely overwhelmed.

My fantasy career had resulted in my

- Being in tremendous debt;
- Working ten to twelve hours a day six days a week; and bringing work home;
- Being responsible for tasks I dreaded;
- Having clients who insisted on speaking only to me;
- Feeling I had no control over my time;
- Lacking the flexibility and freedom to relax when out of the office.

My incentive for becoming self-employed was my naïve expectation that being self-employed would eliminate all my frustrations. I assumed all I had to do was "work hard." I had traded an eight-hour-a-day job for a situation where I had much more responsibility but much less time, money, and freedom. I thought that just because I could sell insurance, I could run an insurance business.

It was that year, 1995, that my business changed—all because of a book I accidentally found at a used bookstore. *E-Myth Revisited* by Michael Gerber was an answer to my prayers. I had originally assumed that I simply needed sales skills to be successful. But as Gerber states, "Just because you understand the technical work of a business doesn't mean you will understand a business that does that technical work." My on-the-job training helped me begin to understand that I needed more employee management skills, financial management skills, and organizational skills.

Mr. Gerber talks about the fact that most people go into business to get rid of the boss. Clearly there is a major flaw in business owners' initial expectations.

Through this book I learned to work "on the business" not just "in the business." I do not personally have to be the one driving the business, but there does need to be a strong structure. I realized it was in everyone's best interest to get the business under control. I learned to restrict my love of "being out of control" mentality to the stable. I was determined to control my business instead of allowing it to control me.

THOUGHT-PROVOKING QUESTIONS AND ACTION PLANS

1. Is the organization you are working in under control? Is it moving proactively and enthusiastically toward clear goals? If not, what steps need to be taken to begin regaining control?

2. Have you read Michael Gerber's book *E-Myth Revisited*? What lessons did you learn from this book? Did you identify with the characters?

3. If you are a business owner, were you initially surprised with the management skills required to run a business (financial, people, legal, operational)? What else about operating a business is different from what you'd expected?

4. Do you currently have employees? If your business does not have employees, it is impossible to clone yourself and gain control. A business without employees is not really a business, it is a job.

5. Do you enjoy being wild and adventurous or must everything run smoothly for you to be happy? Can you see how either extreme can cause frustration for employees and yourself?

Autopilot Leaders Excel

*An autopilot business is propelled to a preset heading by a
clear vision, empowered employees, and supportive systems.*
—Laura Harris

B USINESSES MUST QUICKLY adapt in markets that can be very dynamic.
In order for a business to be successful, everyone inside the system must
want the business to reach success. I want to lead an *autopilot* business. The
word *autopilot* has two primary connotations:

- A person functioning in an unthinking or reflexive manner—
someone who may be walking around in a trance, unaware.

- A person with a clear preset heading—someone who is so deliberate
in his direction that he is not easily sidetracked by obstacles. When
he is thrown off course he realigns quickly because there is a clear
and specific goal.

My business will operate in one of the above manners—reactively with
a lack of direction or proactively with clarity of direction. Most businesses

operate almost by accident. The owner and employees attempt to merely survive eight hours a day with little or no enthusiasm. They are not moving proactively and consistently in a predefined direction.

I once asked a pilot walking through an airport, "Weren't you terrified the first time you put a plane on autopilot?" She immediately responded, "I felt exactly the opposite. I felt so much less stress—even the first time I put the plane on autopilot. I trusted the system."

Now think about a business on autopilot. Wouldn't it be nice to know the team has a clear destination and a desire to work toward it? Wouldn't it be nice to reduce the stress level by creating a situation where you could trust the system?

When I initially opened a business, I could think of only two things— sell something and work long hours. I did not understand the leadership skills I needed to possess or the strategies that the business required.

I began envisioning a business on autopilot. I knew it was possible to design a business that employees and I would enjoy working in. A business on autopilot would need three key components:

- A clear vision of what success looks like
- An empowered team that desires to see the vision become reality
- Strong systems to support the team

A business that is on autopilot allows you to strategically relinquish control to team members while keeping the business on a steady course. It frees the business owner to focus her efforts on the activities that produce the highest return for the business. Having systems in place allows you to be alerted in the event that things are not going as planned. This allows you to reassert control if needed. Autopilot is also wonderful for the employees because with the clarity of direction they have a better understanding of where effort is needed to create success.

Napoleon Hill's book *Think and Grow Rich* describes the importance of "definiteness of purpose." We were working hard but the clear purpose/ vision was missing. Without a clear vision, empowered team, and strong systems, the business would never be on autopilot.

We clearly defined what criteria would create success for our business. We looked at the processes that would have to be in place for us to reach the goals. We determined what training was required to prepare each team member to confidently move toward the goals.

The true test of whether or not we are operating on autopilot is simple. Can the owner or any key person leave for thirty days and the business still move toward the goal in a stress-free manner? Do employees maintain the quality of service, productivity, and profitability regardless of who is present?

Create a self-sufficient business by providing a clear vision, empowering the team, and having strong systems. With an autopilot business the team will have such clarity around the direction that corrections will become automatic if needed. Employees who work in an autopilot business inherently focus on team success. We are totally committed to propelling the company to a preset heading through vision, an empowered team, and strong systems.

THOUGHT-PROVOKING QUESTIONS AND ACTION PLANS

1. During your workday, be conscious of whether or not you are operating in a trance or proactively moving toward a preset heading.

2. Do you feel your behaviors are more like those of a CEO or an employee? Are you really running a business?

3. What activities will you incorporate into your business model that will allow you to become an autopilot leader? Can you paint a clear vision, empower people, and design systems?

4. Does your business have a clear vision of what it takes to be successful? Do you empower the employees to get to the goal? Are systems in place to assure success?

5. When you leave work does your cell phone ring incessantly? Do employees have to call to locate documents? Are you able to relax when you leave the business?

The Power *Is* Not *in the King*

Few things help an individual more than to place responsibility upon him and to let him know that you trust him.
—BOOKER T. WASHINGTON

WHEN I HAD the pleasure of visiting London, a tour guide explained that the kings of the fifteenth and sixteenth centuries had to travel constantly in order to maintain order. They felt the only way to keep their subjects loyal was to be in constant direct contact. Their philosophy was "the power is in the king."

This statement made me reflect on my first years as a business owner. In the early years I felt like I personally had to do almost everything. I was fearful that the customers would feel slighted if I didn't personally assist them (just like the kings did). In addition, the power fed my ego. I thought I was pretty important when I saw my name on a sign for the first time. It felt great to finally be the one in charge.

I became the center of the business by convincing myself that customers might leave if I did not personally handle them. My lack of delegation began to backfire on me. I was insulting my employees by giving them the impression I did not trust them to do their jobs. In addition, they were not learning how to handle challenging situations because I would swoop in and take over. I was convincing our customers that I was the only capable person in the business. Without realizing it, I had created a mindset that "the power is in the queen," namely me.

I now understand that a business cannot be strong if it revolves around the business owner. A strong business owner understands that his or her financial investment is much safer if employees are knowledgeable and if customers can trust them.

Just as the king cannot possibly touch everyone in his kingdom, a business owner cannot be the only long-term point of contact for the customers. Often we need to acknowledge that if we want something done right, we should *not* do it ourselves.

After running the show for a few years, I learned it was not so cool for every client to want to deal with me personally. I was never going to get a life until I improved my delegation skills. I began to study the operation and read books on delegating. Slowly I began to allow others to perform some of my tasks. I no longer jumped in and took over every time a customer called or came in.

I realized that I really wasn't leading if I was unwilling to delegate. Dwight D. Eisenhower said, "Leadership is the ability to decide what is to be done and then get others to want to do it." My employees were capable and willing but I had to delegate the authority and provide training.

In time, employees became very confident in handling basic situations. When the complicated situations arose, I asked guiding questions that would provide employees the confidence to become great problem solvers. They became experts at resolving situations and determining the next steps on their own.

I also had to become comfortable delegating the unpleasant tasks. My instinct was to protect them from any job that might be uncomfortable. It was exhausting to solely handle all of the dirty work. I had to train employees to handle the difficult customers and less pleasant tasks.

An interesting thing happened—I discovered Booker T. Washington was right. My employees did not resent me for expecting them to handle the hard situations; they enjoyed the challenge. Finally, I was making it clear that I had confidence in their abilities.

Obviously it took time to undo the damage I had done with the customers. I had to convince them that not only the "queen" was knowledgeable. I had to build their confidence in the remainder of the team by bragging about them. It took a while but I realized that the customers were much happier when they had full confidence in my employees.

Both our customers and our employees are more satisfied now that I am no longer playing queen. So am I. We operate as a team, and clients understand that they do not have to get to the boss to get exceptional service.

Customers do not care who handles their issues as long as they are resolved efficiently and our service is consistent. Secure leaders give power and energize others. I had finally learned to build a business that did not revolve around me.

THOUGHT-PROVOKING QUESTIONS AND ACTION PLANS

1. Think back to when you were a new business owner. How did it feel to see your name on the sign outside your door?

2. Did you initially assume too much control due to fear of failure? Are you willing to admit the business will be more successful if you empower those around you? Who has the power in your office now? Are you the king or queen?

3. What are three hard tasks or unpleasant interactions that take place in your office? Who is in charge of handling them? Can those tasks be delegated to a well-trained employee? How can you become a delegation expert without dumping all of your work on others?

4. What is your philosophy about delegating? Are there tasks in your operation that only you know how to handle? Is it time to educate at least one other person to handle some of the things you are currently doing?

5. How well does your team respond when you delegate? Take note of what breaks down. What are employees not able to handle? Have you provided the education needed for employees to handle delegated tasks? Do employees have the authority to resolve issues that arise?

6. Are you willing to get tough if you have employees who are not interested in becoming empowered? Can you be patient enough to help them through the transition? Are you self-confident enough to be determined to create a business where employees can handle every situation as well as you can?

You Have Not Earned
the Right to Sleep

You'll have time to rest when you're dead.
—Robert De Niro

T HE FIRST SEVERAL years in business are definitely stressful. I remember numerous sleepless nights, an unfortunate but inevitable consequence of being self-employed.

The excitement attached to growing a business and the heartache that comes with the pressure of the first few years is something I will never forget.

I was reminded of the pain as I delivered a program to business owners in Kansas City, Missouri. At the end of the presentation I asked if there were any questions. A woman raised her hand and began to complain about how difficult it was to run a business. She went on to complain about nights of restless sleep. When I asked how long she had been in business, her response was six months. My immediate counter was "You have not earned the right to sleep."

I knew it sounded harsh. I recalled my sleepless nights and understood her stress. Some stress is natural for a new business owner. But, as a matter of fact, I am much more concerned when a new business owner seems to have no anxiety. Odds are they do not fully comprehend what they have gotten themselves into.

It would have been much easier to allow her to indulge in her pity party. She had expectations of smooth sailing at six months. Unfortunately that was not rational.

Opening a business is not easy. Obstacles are inevitable. A new business owner needs a tremendous resolve to survive the challenges.

I checked on the new business owner three months later and unfortunately found that she had shut down her operation. It crushed me to think of the investment of time and money she had now forgone. Her investment was not going to pay off.

My friend Randy Navarro says, "I want to become an active participant in my own rescue." I love this thought. To survive in business I must be determined to move forward regardless of the difficulties that may arise. I must be willing to sacrifice temporarily and keep focused and positive. I have no time for self-pity. If I must indulge, the "woe is me" mentality needs to be gotten over quickly.

I would not recommend business ownership to anyone who prefers a stress-free life. There is hard work and high stress, especially in the first three to five years. And self-employment is definitely not a "get rich quick" scheme.

Exceptionally successful business owners learn to stay positive and persevere through the inevitable adversity. When I am discouraged I know that meeting with a mastermind group or having lunch with a mentor can get me refocused. A different leadership style is required when the business truly hits adversity. When things are at their worst (market conditions, etc.), three things become extremely important:

- The team needs to be reminded that I will be a strong leader. I need to be optimistic and exude a contagious level of confidence.
- The team must believe that I have their best interests at heart. If they do not trust me or perceive that I do not care about them, momentum will be difficult.

- I must be able to convince the team that I have a plan to overcome, or survive, the adversity. In dire times, the team is even more concerned about a clear plan to attain success.

Communicate, communicate, and communicate. My team is much more likely to stay focused and motivated if they feel they have a clear understanding of the situation. I need to provide two-way communication so that I get a clear picture of their concerns and they get a clear picture of the problem and solution.

Adversity can actually be a blessing. If led appropriately the team can become stronger and more loyal after conquering major adversity. Consider it a challenge and lead in a way that will make your team become excited about overcoming the obstacles.

Stress and hard times are a part of doing business. Because I understood the sacrifice required of a new business owner, I was willing to move forward with sheer determination when the business experienced rough times.

THOUGHT-PROVOKING QUESTIONS AND ACTION PLANS

1. Have you personally experienced any sleepless nights? Are you willing to deal with the stress and put in the hours required to run a successful business?

2. How can you create a mentality that failure is not an option? Journaling can relieve some of the anxiety and keep you focused. Yes, I write in a diary daily.

3. Make a list of the reasons you started your own business. Revisit the list when you get discouraged. A quick reminder of the long-term advantages can help you stay focused when the going gets tough.

4. Who are some of your heroes? What adversities did they overcome to reach their goals? Use their stories to remind you that success is not defined by the lack of adversity but by a person's resolve to overcome adversity.

5. Find a local mentor who can keep you motivated when you run into daily obstacles. Commit to challenging each other and holding each other accountable for progress in your business and personal lives.

6. Do you adapt your leadership style when times are hard? Does your team feel confident that you can lead them through the difficult times?

Lead Me and Manage Me

Management is a process of assuring that the program and objectives of the organization are implemented. Leadership on the other hand has to do with casting vision and motivating people.
—JOHN MAXWELL

S OME INDIVIDUALS LOVE looking at a business holistically and determining what needs to be done. Others prefer to be involved in the execution and derive pleasure from seeing a plan come to fruition. Would you rather be a good leader or a good manager? An organization needs both skills to operate on all cylinders. I need to evaluate my skills on a regular basis to make sure we do not overemphasize one or the other.

Leaders proactively concentrate on the horizon whereas managers are more likely to focus on the details of today. As Steven Covey says, "Management works in the system; leadership works on the system." Throughout the day I stop and think . . . am I spending enough time working in my business and on my business?

Leadership is about influencing people, managing dreams, obtaining commitment, taking risks, and earning trust. Using storytelling abilities, leaders paint a picture of the long-term vision. Thriving on personal power, they inspire change and motivate others, often through their charismatic personality.

Managers execute tasks, control operational issues, and wield positional power, often implementing the vision of another. They prefer status quo, often enjoy stability, resist change, and prefer to reduce risk and thrive on efficiency.

Ideally I instinctively know when it is appropriate to behave more like a leader and when my management skills should be utilized. I need strength in leadership and management and the ability to toggle back and forth throughout the day. The key is determining the right balance. I must use leadership skills to guide the team through the creation of a clear vision. I need management skills to make sure the vision becomes reality.

A strong leader will be able to connect emotionally to the group, listen well, have a strong sense of self, and be willing to be a nonconformist. A strong manager will have insight into the organization and its processes. He/she will be knowledgeable on the details of the operation and controlling organizational resources. Kenneth E. Clark and Miriam B. Clark state, "The exercise of leadership accomplishes goals more effectively than the usual management methods of trading rewards for performance."

Without strong leadership skills, team members will be less likely to buy into the long-term vision of my organization. If I am a weak leader employees will have little desire to work toward the goal or show loyalty. The confidence and skills of the business owner will determine the momentum of the team. I need to create an atmosphere of achievement.

It has been said that one is leading only if someone is following. I must be willing to determine whether or not my current leadership style is energizing or draining those around me. Leadership is not a title. Leaders and managers emerge at every level of an organization. Some leaders are appointed while other leaders emerge naturally because of their influence on the team. My team will function best if I share responsibility and improve leadership skills at every level of the organization.

Ideally you will build a team of professionals and develop their leadership and management skills. A self-confident business owner will encourage team members to show initiative. A strong leader will create a sense of confidence and trust throughout the organization.

Dr. Warren Bennis alleges, "Failing organizations are usually over-managed and under-led." It is easy to get caught up in your day-to-day operation and lose track of the importance of being a leader. You need strong leadership and management skills to create a strong vision and execute it.

THOUGHT-PROVOKING QUESTIONS AND ACTION PLANS

1. Do your employees draw strength from you? Do you transfer confidence to them?

2. Do you take the time to get to know your employees individually? Do your employees know that you care about them? Do they trust you and believe you have their best interest at heart? If they aren't following, you aren't leading.

3. Are you supportive when change is necessary? Are you able to paint a picture that inspires the team to adapt quickly?

4. Do you spend a proper amount of time with people and processes? Overemphasis on leadership skills can lead to not accomplishing your daily tasks. Overemphasis on management can kill morale.

5. Do you encourage leadership development of personnel at all levels? Do employees see that the organization is committed to their personal development?

Who Is Serving Whom?

The first responsibility of a leader is to define reality. The last is to say thank you. In between, the leader is a servant.
—MAX DU PREE

ONE OF THE advantages of being a business owner is that you *get* to be the boss. One of the disadvantages of being a business owner is that you *have* to be the boss. We have all heard the old adage "Do onto others as you would have them do unto you." The "Golden Rule," as it is called, is a pretty simple concept. We should attempt to treat others the way we would like to be treated. This concept applies to every aspect of our lives but it is not always easy to live by.

A tremendous amount has been written about the concept of servant leadership, which is radically different from the typical hierarchical system. Team members will seldom follow a leader long term merely because of the power the title imposes. Servant leaders, however, realize that more is accomplished through collaboration than coercion.

Servant leadership can be demonstrated in many ways:

- Design the business so that you seem approachable. Make sure that the location of your office is not isolated to emphasize your importance. The furniture in your office should not be much more expensive than in other offices to signify that you are more important than your employees.

- Take on the difficult as well as the pleasant tasks. A servant leader is one who is willing to live down in the trenches with the team. No task is beneath her. Design each person's job so that she is working within her strengths and distribute the workload fairly.

- Make sure your daily behaviors indicate that you are all equal. Be willing to sit down in an employee's space to discuss things that come up during the day instead of summoning employees into your office. Acknowledge teammates on a regular basis, genuinely indicating that you care about them. E. M. Kelly described the difference between a boss and a leader: "A boss says, 'Go!' A leader says, 'Let's go!'"

- Make sure your language indicates that you are a servant leader. When you refer to employees, avoid words that indicate they are less valuable (*secretary*, *receptionist*) and use instead words like *assistant* or *teammate*.

- When referring to the business, don't emphasize the fact that you are the owner. Don't tell customers to call only you when they have a question; make it known that everyone is knowledgeable.

- Be sure that the advertising and marketing is not about you but about the team. Make it reinforce the concept that you are a group of experts.

- Stifle your inordinate need to be heard, and don't talk more than you listen. Be willing to allow others an opportunity to share ideas.

- Be friendly with employees without causing complication by becoming embroiled in their personal lives.

- Be willing to help someone who has absolutely no ability to further your career. Samuel Johnson said, "The true measure of a man is how he treats someone who can do him absolutely no good."

- Create an organization where the owner, employees, and customers can all succeed simultaneously. Align objectives appropriately, and be sure to build leadership skills of employees at all levels.

You must remain continually focused on ways in which you can serve those around you. Robert Greenleaf said, "Good leaders must first become good servants." Your business will be strong if you look for ways to serve employees and customers. You will also find that leadership is much more enjoyable when you are a servant leader.

As Max Du Pree indicated, we are to define reality, serve others, then remember to say thank you. A leader's treatment of employees determines how employees will treat customers. Look for ways to be a servant leader by putting yourself aside and helping others get ahead.

THOUGHT-PROVOKING QUESTIONS AND ACTION PLANS

1. Do you express a genuine care and concern for those that you work with? Can they tell that you care about them?

2. Are you willing to get down in the trenches and do the dirty work with your employees or do you delegate out all of the unpleasant tasks? Are you too important to make the coffee or replace the water bottle at the cooler in your office? Are you willing to get your hands dirty? How can you communicate by your actions, not words, that you do not consider yourself more important?

3. Do you trust that your employees will do what is best for the business? Allow them to earn the trust, then acknowledge their value to the organization. Do you recognize employees when they go above and beyond the call of duty?

4. Do you allow employees to have time off when there are crucial family matters that need to be addressed? Do you do it without making them feel guilty?

Mentors Accelerate Growth

Mentor: Someone whose hindsight can become your foresight.
—AUTHOR UNKNOWN

As a new business owner I was constantly seeking out the advice of more seasoned business owners. I made a list of the most successful business owners in my industry. When I was in their areas, I would ask if I could personally observe their operations.

The vast majority were extremely generous and invited me to "come on over." Many of these business owners have now become close friends. In fact, over the years I visited hundreds of businesses. Only three business owners declined the request to share business practices with me.

I was overwhelmed by most entrepreneurs' willingness to share their expertise. I am convinced their willingness to share is part of their success.

Questions I typically ask seasoned business owners include:

- What motivates you?

- Do you set goals? If so, how?
- What was the biggest challenge when you started your business?
- What is your biggest challenge today?
- What made you decide to go into this industry?
- What template do you use for a business plan?
- How can I learn what I need to know about this profession?
- What are the three key attributes to being successful in this field?
- If you were going to start all over again, what specific steps would you take?
- Do you know anybody in this profession, or in any other, that you would recommend I talk to?
- How are responsibilities divided in your business?
- What is the source of most of your new business sales?
- How do you improve customer loyalty?
- How do you balance your business goals and personal goals?
- What are the steps you go through in hiring?
- What is the biggest mistake you ever made in business?
- What makes your business exceptional?
- What books have you read that have had the biggest impact on your career?

Always have a pencil and paper in hand when speaking with a mentor. Take lots of notes and then study the information later. Contemplate what changes, if any, should be made. How will your business be different because of the things you learned?

I was shocked to discover that business owners do not always clearly understand what makes their operation so successful. They may not understand what makes them unique. I discovered that I had to not only ask the right questions but I also had to become extremely intuitive while I was observing the operation.

A mentor can radically reduce a learning curve. Mentoring others can reduce the learning curve also. I often mentor others. Their questions frequently spark thoughts that provide additional ways to improve my business.

As I assist others I am reminded of the lessons I learned. I have also found that when I mentor others I hold myself to a higher standard.

Take shortcuts by learning from others' mistakes. I was blessed to learn from others' mistakes and, therefore, reduce the number I made myself. Be grateful to those who are willing to give and generously give to others.

THOUGHT-PROVOKING QUESTIONS AND ACTION PLANS

1. Do you have a mentor? What is one specific thing she has suggested that has benefited you in some way?

2. Have you ever visited other businesses to observe their operations? If so, what is one idea you've implemented? How did that improve the way you did business?

3. Did you ever receive bad advice from someone? Did you take it at face value and act on it without taking your situation into account?

4. Have you thanked a mentor for sharing his hard-earned wisdom? How have you let him know that his contribution has made a difference for you?

5. Have you returned the favor and functioned as a mentor for someone else? How can you formally or informally share the knowledge you have with others?

Do Not Avoid Fear . . . Attack It

You gain strength, courage, and confidence by every experience in which you really stop to look fear in the face. You must do the thing you cannot do.
— Eleanor Roosevelt

THINK BACK TO your earliest fear. My first traumatic experience happened in first grade when my teacher asked me to take a pair of scissors to another classroom. Seems mundane, right? I remember feeling proud in being chosen to deliver the scissors to the neighboring classroom. But I would soon regret the confidence my teacher had placed in me.

Walking into the classroom was uneventful until I reached the front of the room. I looked up at the teacher and handed her the scissors (you guessed it!), pointed end toward her. The teacher educated the entire room on the "dangers" of inappropriately handling scissors. After scolding me she insisted I walk back to my teacher, explain what I had done, then return and hand her the scissors correctly. Argh!!! Had I not been six I would have run away. I can still remember how the silence surrounded me as I returned to the room for a second time.

My emotion went from beaming pride to complete confusion in mere seconds. The way she handled the situation left a lasting impression. I survived but learned to dread being the center of attention.

I had an equally appalling situation on my thirteenth birthday, when I was forced to do a presentation in front of my class as punishment for not knowing the significance of Pearl Harbor. Memories of my first-grade horror flooded back as I gave the oral report. I made up my mind in that instant that I would never again be forced to speak in front of a group. I made it through the remainder of my schooling without ever having to speak publicly.

Fast-forward from age thirteen to age thirty-seven, when I was asked by a friend to share business practices in front of a group of business owners. My immediate reaction was simple—*no way!* After tremendous coaxing, I reluctantly agreed to speak on two conditions:

- I would not stand to speak.
- The group had to be small.

They agreed to my silly demands. I worried myself sick prior to the event. The meeting went well but I was exhausted due to my self-imposed stress. Later I contemplated how juvenile my fears were. They were, however, very real to me. I became determined to overcome the anxiety that public speaking created.

I began forcing myself to speak in front of groups when asked. I attended seminars that featured the best professional speakers and watched closely to determine what characteristics made some speakers exceptional. I eventually hired a speaking coach and did the assigned homework.

I read Roger Ailes's *You Are the Message* and *Speak and Grow Rich* by Dottie Walters, and I enjoyed learning to turn my fear into an asset. I learned that knowledge eradicates fear. The more I studied public speaking, the more comfortable I became.

Three years later I became the president of a local club, Toastmasters International, which improves public-speaking skills. Furthermore, I joined the National Speakers Association and took a leadership position in the club. Instead of dreading public speaking, I decided to conquer it!

Today I am most at home, most authentic and honest, when I am sharing in front of a group. When teaching programs on improving communication skills and mentoring new speakers, I am completely vulnerable. My audience understands that I have personally experienced the fears that some of them are struggling with. I receive tremendous gratification from teaching that which was hardest for me to learn. Tackling my fears gave me leadership skills and confidence. I have proven that we can grow and change—it is a choice.

I made a list of "101 Things I Want to Do Before I Die." It includes dreams such as traveling to Greece and taking my nieces, nephews, and granddaughter to Disney World.

Then I added to the list everything I was afraid of. My list includes skydiving, obtaining a motorcycle license, whitewater rafting, and going on a mission trip to a foreign country. I gain confidence as I tackle the things that terrify me, one at a time.

M. Scott Peck said, "The truth is that our finest moments are most likely to occur when we are feeling deeply uncomfortable, unhappy, or unfulfilled. For it is only in such moments, propelled by our discomfort, that we are likely to step out of our ruts and start searching for different ways or truer answers."

THOUGHT-PROVOKING QUESTIONS AND ACTION PLANS

1. Do any of your fears have power over you? Is there still a fear of public speaking, meeting strangers, heights, or swimming? Make a list of at least ten things that you won't do because of fear. Pick one item to tackle every six to twelve months. Living in fear is optional—opt out!

2. Find an expert on a subject that you fear. Ask for advice on overcoming your fear. Most people are very willing to share if you are respectful of their time. If you need additional one-on-one assistance, take a course on the subject.

3. Fears are often magnified by lack of understanding. Read about the subject you fear. Ask your mentor/expert what books he/she would recommend you read.

4. Do fears or insecurities affect any portion of your business? Are there fears of relinquishing control, financial fears, or fear of prospecting? Do you become paralyzed with new technology and allow others to be the expert for you?

Get Happy or Get Gone

To love what you do and feel that it
matters, what could be more fun?
—KATHARINE GRAHAM

I HEARD A SAYING years ago, "If you want to be happy for a day, win the lottery. If you want to be happy for life, do what you love." I wholeheartedly agree. A common characteristic of exceptionally successful people is they love what they do. Ideally we each design a business where we blur the line between work and play.

I recall a specific time when I did not enjoy my job. I was overwhelmed and could not get excited about work. My emotions eventually translated to spending less time getting dressed up in the mornings. I was exhausted and burned out. I did not want to spend time on my appearance. I did not work fewer hours but I was less enthusiastic and did not dress like the consummate professional.

I was careful to dress within the guidelines of the employee handbook, which was fairly lenient. It merely stated that we could not wear blue jeans, shorts, or tennis shoes to work. Instead of suits, I began wearing khakis and a dress shirt with our company logo.

Within weeks there was a noticeable drop in the enthusiasm level throughout the office. No one was dressing professionally. I wasn't, so why should they? I had not verbally communicated my burnout but the nonverbal message was clearly having a negative effect on morale. Furthermore, this nonchalant attitude had extended to our productivity. We were not getting as much work done and sales were down. It seemed our casual attire was transferring itself into a casual attitude about work. It never occurred to me that dressing in a less than professional manner and not being enthusiastic would have such a negative impact on the team.

I made the decision to energize the team instead of draining it. I made a point to dress as a consummate professional. As I improved my appearance and made an effort to be more enthusiastic at work, I truly became happier. Almost immediately I could tell a difference in the energy level of the employees. Their behavior modeled mine; when mine was good, theirs was good, and vice versa.

I often ask clients, "Why do you do business with our firm?" It is an informal way of identifying what we are doing right. The most frequent response to that question is "I can tell you love what you do." I even had one gentleman say, "Obviously you guys love what you do, that's weird." In a strange way, I knew that was a compliment. Consumers are not used to dealing with businesses that act enthusiastic and eager to please. People respond very positively when you have a genuine passion for life.

I am not a Pollyanna. There are certainly days when I do not absolutely love going to work. There are days when I am preoccupied about something going on in my personal life. On those days, I stop before I walk into the office and put on my "game face." I tell myself, "Get happy or get gone." I am serious. If I cannot turn around my attitude then I should not walk into the office. Others should not have to be around me.

The steps I go through when I am having a bad day are to

- Acknowledge my moody behavior—do a gut check.
- Have a "spoil me" activity. I love to relax with a Dr Pepper or take a brief walk outdoors.
- Put on a smile and get on with my life.

By pretending we are happy we are much more likely to start feeling that way. I use the old adage—fake it until you make it. The very act of putting a smile on our face helps us get out of that blue mood. A negative attitude is a choice.

Recently I was sitting at my desk reminiscing about how I loved climbing trees as a child. I had not been up in a tree in more than thirty years. I walked out of the office in the middle of the day and climbed up into a tree in front of our building. I sat up there for twenty minutes and thanked God for everything that was right in my life.

I might have looked very silly but I enjoyed taking a moment to concentrate on everything that was positive. It's sometimes easier to concentrate on the negative aspects of life. Now periodically I remind myself that I don't have to climb up into a tree to remember to count my blessings and get happy.

I would love to have contagious enthusiasm personally and professionally. As Michel Fortin said, "Do what you love and the business will follow."

THOUGHT-PROVOKING QUESTIONS AND ACTION PLANS

1. Are there days you dread going to work? How do you think your negative attitude affects those you work with?

2. What are you going to do next time you are in a foul mood? How are you going to turn it around?

3. Do you love what you do or do you feel buried under all your obligations? Do you walk around with a grim expression on your face? Do you realize that what you are feeling is what you are projecting?

4. What is one specific thing you do to make work more meaningful and fun for yourself and your employees?

5. Do you require that employees "get happy or get gone"? Are there employees in your operation who seem to be perpetually unhappy? Have you created an atmosphere where fellow employees have to walk on eggshells when either you or a fellow teammate chooses to have a bad day?

Move On or Move On

When I argue with reality I lose, but only 100 percent of the time.
—Byron Katie

A S A CHILD my favorite board game was Candyland. The board was so colorful and the gingerbread men so cute. Running a business can be like Candyland; you get the impression you are winning and then suddenly, fate sends you back ten steps. As a child I would get frustrated but eventually came to understand that setbacks were an inevitable part of playing the game.

As adults we can become paralyzed with frustration when circumstances force us back a few steps. Our reaction to these inevitable setbacks determines whether or not we obtain long-term success. Life is full of frustrations. At times we will create a clear picture in our mind of how things will go. When reality does not coincide with our dream we can become disheartened. Unmet expectations can cause frustration.

It is easy to become frustrated when an expected result does not come to pass. When a situation seems to be going south, typically only one or two people have the ability to resolve the issue. At times no one has the ability to make things go the way we believe they should.

Early in my career a mentor listened patiently as I complained about a situation that I felt was unfair. He quietly allowed me to carry on regarding the perceived injustice. I used him as a sounding board while attempting to analyze the situation from every angle. After complaining for an extended period of time and getting myself completely riled up, I begged for advice.

He calmly asked, "Laura, is there anything you can do to change the situation?" After some thought, my response was a resigned, "No." Dwight replied with "Then suck it up and get on with your life."

I was shocked. I expected sympathy. I was enjoying my pity party. Dwight was not concerned about providing an unpopular stance. He was right; there was no point in worrying about things I could not control. My passion was not going to change the situation; it would only feed my frustration. By refusing to let go, I was making the situation worse.

There have been times when I have felt frustrated or overwhelmed because of legislative constraints in my industry. There have been situations when I felt competitors were unethical in their behavior. I have occasionally felt unappreciated or betrayed by an employee that I cared deeply for. There were times when I invested large sums of monies in an advertising campaign that provided no return. Life is not always fair. I realized that there is a right way and a wrong way to handle myself when I am irritated with a situation that is out of my control.

My brother Greg has a clear perspective on this. One of the many reasons I love Greg is he does not say much unless it is profound. I once explained a situation to Greg that I perceived to be unfair. When I finally quieted he said "Laura, when something is not handled the way you choose, you have two options: you can move on (let it go emotionally) or you can move on (remove yourself from the situation)."

It was so simple yet so wise. Once a situation becomes inoperable, I need to let it go. Greg and Dwight allowed me to see there is no point in focusing on situations that I do not have the power to change.

If I bring a concern and a suggested solution to the individual in charge and he or she chooses to brush me off, I need to "move on" or "move on." There is no point in allowing myself to remain frustrated once a decision is final.

I also need to be careful about associating regularly with those who habitually whine about things that are outside of their control. I need to remove myself from the situation completely. I have been around business owners who constantly focus on the negative. This is not prison. I am free and I do have the option of completely removing myself from my current situation.

When I am emotional about a perceived injustice, I find I am more effective when I invoke the "48-hour rule." I wait forty-eight hours before bringing the issue to the person in charge. After giving myself a chance to think, I have a clearer and more rational idea of the proper action.

Don't become paralyzed when things are not going your way. Maya Angelou said, "If you don't like something, change it. If you can't change it, change your attitude. Don't complain." Good advice. Bounce back quickly when things are not going your way.

THOUGHT-PROVOKING QUESTIONS AND ACTION PLANS

1. Do you find yourself coming from a "lack" mentality? Do you focus on negative things that are outside of your control? How does that impact you and the people around you?

2. What are the issues that are bothering you right now? Do you have the power to change them? If so, how are you going to fix the course for the future instead of complaining?

3. If you do not have the authority to resolve an issue, who does? Who "owns" this situation and has the authority to improve it? How are you going to approach that person to try to resolve the issue?

4. Determining who has responsibility for the issue you are concerned about does not assure you will have satisfactory resolution. What are you going to do if the person in charge does not take what you consider the "appropriate" action? Will you argue with reality?

5. Are you willing to forgive and forget when someone hurts your feelings or handles a situation in a less than ideal manner? Are you wasting energy by remaining frustrated with someone?

You Are the Average of
Your Five Closest Friends

Our chief want in life is for someone to make us do what we can.
—Ralph Waldo Emerson

As an autopilot leader I am surrounded by employees whom I enjoy working with. A lot of my daily social interaction is with my fellow teammates. When I leave the office I have a choice as to whom I will spend my time with. I am blessed to be surrounded by friends who have taught me a lot. Those friendships can provide an outlet when I need to be energized. They can also challenge me to stay focused on continually becoming a better person and boss.

I was listening to a speaker talk about friendships several years ago. She suggested we should be very careful in determining whom we would spend time with. I immediately stopped and analyzed my current relationships. Were the people that I spend time with energizing me or draining me? Were they challenging me to be a better person?

Eventually I began considering whether or not there were any relationships that had a negative impact on my life. For a moment I realized that I was actually considering which friends might need to be thrown by the wayside. Finally my brain skipped to the next step. Which of my friends might be contemplating discarding me as they listened to the same speech? Scary!!!

We have such a finite amount of time on this earth. Where we spend that time and with whom is crucial. We have typically either consciously or unconsciously chosen our closest friends. I am convinced that the caliber of people we surround ourselves with affects who we become.

I am not recommending that you stop affiliating with family or current friends. I am not recommending that you don't associate with people who don't have it all together.

I do try to seek out friendships and spend the majority of my time with people that will challenge me to become a better person because . . .

- If I have friends that are positive, I will become a more positive person.
- If I have friends that are giving, I will likely become a more generous person.
- If I have friends that are focused, I will become a more focused person.
- If I have friends that are ambitious, I will be more likely to strive to be the best.
- If I have friends that have balanced lives, I will be reminded to be a balanced person.

Find mentors and make friends who will educate and challenge you. Gravitate to those who will hold your feet to the fire and give you courage. We need friends who will stretch us and call us on the carpet when needed.

My closest friends have very different strengths and weaknesses. I respect them because of their spiritual maturity, devotion to family, business acumen, commitment to personal development, generous hearts, and love of adventure. They bring out the best in me and I want to be a person that brings out the best in them.

Keep in mind that not everyone will support you if you dream big. At times even friends and family may not be supportive.

Bruce Wilkinson describes an interesting concept called "dream bullies" in his book *The Dream Giver*. He points out that not everyone will encourage you as you dream big. He discusses the importance of moving forward toward your dreams even when others intentionally or unintentionally discourage you. Surround yourself with the right people but know that you are ultimately responsible for your success.

Ulysses S. Grant once said, "I was successful because you believed in me." Associate with those who will challenge you and call you on the carpet when you are moving in the wrong direction. Be a person who brings out the best in others. The caliber of people whom we surround ourselves with affects who we become.

It is also nice to seek out friendships with those who have strengths to offset our weaknesses. We need to find mentors and coaches or create mastermind groups that will push us to become better people. I need to be surrounded with a diverse group of well-rounded individuals.

When I opened my business I asked a businessman what a reasonable sales goal was for my first year. He gave me a number and that became our goal. Twelve months later I learned how ridiculously low our expectations had been. The goal he provided, though not deceptive, turned out to be extremely unambitious. Unfortunately I was limited for an entire year by low expectations that had been set by someone else. As the saying goes, "Free advice is sometimes worth what we pay for it."

Eventually I met business owners with much higher aspirations and our production increased 250 percent within sixty days without adding any processes or staff. We simply discarded our preconceived notion of acceptable production.

I no longer blindly accept advice I receive as gospel. I listen to everyone, being careful to seek out opinions of the most successful business owners. Then I make a decision with well-rounded information.

It has been said that good judgment comes from experience and experience comes from poor judgment. Failure is inevitable. The people in history who have become icons in leadership have made plenty of mistakes and bold endeavors. Often they are driven by their passions to move with reckless abandon toward specific goals.

THOUGHT-PROVOKING QUESTIONS AND ACTION PLANS

1. Make a list of the five people you spend the most time with (outside of your family). Determine whether or not these are people who help you grow.

2. Try to seek out people to spend time with who have the same core values as yours. Look for those with personality strengths in areas where you want to build your character. Who would that be?

3. Have you ever lost a friend because they became insecure with your personal growth? Unfortunately not everyone will support your goals. Be conscious as to whether or not the relationships you have are positively impacting your life.

4. The influence that you have on others comes with a responsibility. Are you the type of friend who challenges others to become better or one who brings others down? Ask your friends.

5. Have you become complacent in some area of your life? Do you need a friend to motivate you to be a better businessperson, take better care of your body, or become more active in giving to the community? Determine who is strong where you are weak and see if that person will become your accountability partner.

Do Not Prop Your Feet Up

When influencing others, example is not the
main thing. It is the only thing.
—ALBERT SCHWEITZER

I MET AN INDIVIDUAL several years ago who opened a business because
he wanted to be a boss. Apparently that is *all* he wanted to do. He had
visions of sitting with his feet propped up on his aircraft carrier–sized desk,
smoking a cigar, and counting the money as it poured in.

Within six months his savings were gone and he was out of business.
Once you have a million customers you may have the luxury of basking in
your role as captain. Prior to that, business owners do not have the luxury of
delegating 100 percent of their work.

My employees will never put more effort into the business than they see
me putting forth. Based on the amount of effort I am putting into my career,
would I hire me?

I set the tempo and work ethic for the office. Like it or not, I teach with
my life, not my words. My employees will not follow what I say; they will
emulate my behavior. I have to work the way I want the team to work. If I

do not stay focused on income-producing activities, neither will anyone else. Guess who had better be the hardest-working person in the office? *Me!*

In addition, everyone—including the business owner—must be engaged in activities that generate income. This is especially crucial when the business is new. I personally need to be generating income. It is important that I manage employees but that activity seldom generates immediate income.

The formula is pretty simple. In most businesses, if I am not selling something or improving customer retention, I am not generating income.

In addition to being a leader, I should also be the following:

Lead Generator I must have a clear marketing program in place to attract the ideal customer. They will not come running in when we open the door. Some business owners hire employees, hand them a phone, and say, "Good luck." If an employee wanted that stress, she would open her own business. As the business owner, I am primarily responsible for deciding what processes should be put in place to solicit new customers.

Salesperson Once processes are designed, my employees and I must spend the day drumming up business. Proactively commit to specific sales goals. Talk to people in person and on the phone. Invoke the "Three-Foot Rule." If someone comes within three feet of you, explain that you are a new business owner and would like the opportunity to earn their business. This rule applies to every person on the payroll; if you are receiving a paycheck—you are in sales.

Trainer There must always be a mentality of continuous education throughout the organization. I prefer to personally train new employees whenever possible. If I do the initial training of each person, then I know the basics are consistent throughout the organization. As I work hard to build this business I must clone myself.

Last weekend I was speaking to a new business owner. She bragged that she opened a new business so she could arrange her schedule to spend most of her time at home with her children. She admitted that she typically was in the office for only two hours a day and the business would fall apart if she lost her key employee. She is not only failing to contribute to the bottom line, but her business is also very vulnerable.

Delegating is a key part of making a new business work but abdicating responsibility is a formula for disaster. Be careful not to take delegating to an extreme. You need to always remain focused on finding ways to drive customers into the business and improve customer loyalty. Your behavior should be a clear picture of what you desire from your teammates. You need to hold yourself accountable and pull your weight in lieu of attempting to delegate all tasks.

THOUGHT-PROVOKING QUESTIONS AND ACTION PLANS

1. Have you ever seen a business owner who thought he could hire others to do all the work while he sat back and acted important? What effect did that have on the employees?

2. Do you struggle most with drumming up the business or closing the deal? Do you waste money because you enjoy the activities that get the phone to ring but prefer not to do the paperwork? What is one specific step you are going to take this week to become more committed to lead generation and sales?

3. How are you going to generate more leads? How are you going to set a positive example? Will you stay focused so employees follow your lead?

4. Are you committed to continually improving the education level of employees or do you prefer to focus only on sales? Have you created an organization where employees enjoy learning? Are the basic operations performed consistently throughout the organization?

5. Does everyone within the organization understand that they must generate new business? Are you or any employee in your organization considered administration and, therefore, exempt from sales? Why would you have a person in your operation who is not responsible for contributing to the sales goals?

Exercise Is Not a Luxury

If you don't take care of your body, where will you live?
—Sign in gym

OPENING A NEW business is similar to going off to college. Just as many students gain the freshman fifteen the first year away from home, many new business owners also pack on the pounds. My first year as a business owner, I gained weight! I had been warned about the fifteen-pound rule, but I didn't take the warning seriously.

Then reality hit. As a new business owner I imposed a lot of pressure on myself to produce immediate results. I would become so engrossed in my job that I frequently worked through lunch. Many times my staff and I were on a roll and did not stop to take a break. One of us would make a trip to a local fast-food restaurant and buy lunch for everyone. We would eat at our desk and make phone calls simultaneously.

We drank a ridiculous number of soft drinks throughout the day. Each of us typically had a soda on our desk at any given moment. Exercise was not an afterthought—it was not a thought, period! Sleep was erratic, at best. We had our blinders on and were focused on success.

I was operating long hours with lots of caffeine, inadequate sleep, and no exercise. It took me months to recognize what a toll this was taking on my energy level and effectiveness. I was very excited about our goals but I was burned out.

I realized that I needed to establish guidelines and boundaries about taking care of myself. I had to prioritize my health—or I would not be effective in business—by

- Doing my best to adhere to consistent sleep patterns.
- Getting out of the office for lunch.
- Deciding not to work all night and day. There will *always* be more work to be done. If I think, "I will go home as soon as I get everything finished," I will never leave.
- Bringing healthy snacks to the office. Fast food seldom provides healthy options.
- Using teammates to hold me accountable for a healthy lifestyle.
- Determining that physical exercise was not optional. There will never be "extra time." I must make time.

I needed to make sure I was not living a lopsided life. I didn't want to be all work and no play.

We all know that there are two primary components to having a healthy lifestyle—eat right and move more. We are not meant to be sedentary. Exercise is not a luxury. It will never be convenient so it had better be a priority.

I began really paying attention to the leaders of major corporations. I noticed that often the majority of these CEOs appeared to be very healthy. I began to wonder if there was a correlation between taking care of my health and being successful in business. Seldom did I see someone who was extremely successful and clearly unhealthy.

After the terrorists attacked on September 11, 2001, I watched a CNN news anchor provide an update while President Bush did his morning jog. I was shocked! How did he have time to run? I couldn't find time and I had minor problems compared to the issues he was dealing with.

That is the day I decided healthy living is a choice. I had to pick something I enjoyed. If I was merely forcing myself to exercise, it would be hard to make myself be disciplined enough to continue long term. I chose yoga, Tae Kwon Do, and horseback riding to provide exercise and enjoyment.

I have personally seen that I am more effective at work and absolutely make more income when I take care of myself. The increased energy level alone is tremendous. I am happier at home and at work. When I take care of my health, I maximize wealth.

THOUGHT-PROVOKING QUESTIONS AND ACTION PLANS

1. Do you exercise on a regular basis? What positive impact does it have on your life? Does it increase your energy level at work? Identify a physical activity that you love. It could be racquetball, jazz dance, gardening, or aerobics. Schedule it into your calendar.

2. Do you limit the number of hours employees are expected to work? What strategies can you put in place that will keep everyone from getting burned out?

3. Do you or your employees eat at your desk? Do staff members frequently bring in fast food or unhealthy snacks? How does this affect the office energy level?

4. Have you or other employees gained weight recently? Is it due to poor habits or stress? How can you support each other in maintaining a healthy lifestyle?

5. What tricks have you learned to help stay in the habit of working out? Try putting your exercise program in your daily calendar, laying out your exercise clothes the night before, having a workout buddy, or having extra bottles of water in your car before you leave for work.

Stop Speeding Through Life

I can't talk right now, Grandma, I'm really
busy. I'll have to call you back later.
—Jaquelyn Trave' Stokes (my two-year-old granddaughter)

THE QUOTE ABOVE is real. The very first time my granddaughter called me she was not quite three years old. Unfortunately I was on an airplane so I did not catch the call. I was overjoyed to the point of tears as I listened to her message asking me to call her.

When the plane landed, even before getting my luggage, I called her in Miami. When she answered the phone I anxiously said, "Jaquelyn, this is Grandma." Her response was the above quote. The two-year-old was too busy to talk. In shock I jokingly responded, "No, Jaquelyn Trave', this is your grandma and you will speak to me right now." Her chipper response was "Okay, Grandma."

The situation is hysterical now but at the time it reminded me that we live in a society that has made it fashionable to be busy. Undoubtedly, Jackie had heard "I'm busy" enough times in her two years to deduce that it was "cool" to be busy.

A friend and I were listening to the radio at work several years ago when a song by the group Alabama came on the radio. The lead lyric in the song was "I'm in a hurry to get things done, Oh I rush and rush until life's no fun." My friend turned to me and said, "That should be your theme song." I knew she was right and unfortunately I somewhat prided myself on having a Type A, spastic personality. How insane!

Many of us have to make a conscious effort to relax. I often rush to my appointments frazzled and out of breath. One day I ran to an appointment for a massage. As I calmed down and took a breath my massage therapist said, "If the police gave tickets for speeding through life, you would not be able to afford insurance."

Hmmm. Do you think my friends were trying to tell me something?

Being driven is wonderful for accomplishing tasks. I have to make a conscious effort to slow down. I decided to arrive thirty minutes before the office opened and plan out each day. This planning time allows me to be pro-active and organized. I became methodical instead of manic. When I leave work at the end of the day I have the satisfaction of knowing I typically accomplished the most important things.

The late great actor Glenn Ford said, "If they try to rush me I always say, 'I've only got one other speed—and it's slower.'" That's what planning my time does for me. It helps me slow down instead of speeding through the day.

The constant consolidating monster was not limited to the office. It came out when I was with my family and friends as well.

One day my teenage daughter and I were driving to Padre Island to ride horses. When we got in the car she immediately opened her cell phone and began visiting with friends. I was thrilled because I realized that since she was on the phone I would have time to make a few calls. I picked up my phone and was determined to accomplish as much as possible in the short drive.

After the third or fourth call, I realized that Kara was quiet. I looked at her and saw tears in her eyes. My mind was racing. Had some boy been mean, some girl been catty? Why was she so upset? I got off the phone immediately and gave her a puzzled look. She said, "Even when I get your time, I can't get your attention."

Out of the mouths of babes . . . She was right. There are times when it is not acceptable to multitask. I was trying to mark two things off my to-do list at once.

I decided that when I was with my daughters, I was going to be with my daughters, period. I was no longer going to send the message "Work is my priority."

Most of us are juggling many responsibilities. It is easy to rush through the day or give half an ear while someone is talking to us. We may be physically present but have mentally moved on to something else.

I learned a technique from my friend Sam Horn, who wrote a book on communication called *Tongue Fu!* She says the word *listen* contains the same letters as the word *silent* for good reason. Sam says authentic listening can be improved if we do the following:

Look the other person in the eye. M. Scott Peck says, "You cannot truly listen to anyone and do anything else at the same time." If you are answering emails and a client or employee wants to talk to you, turn away from the computer. If you are reading or doing paperwork, put your book or files down on the desk. By putting away what you were doing and looking people in the eye, you are sending the message "You are more important than this. It can wait."

Lift your eyebrows. Try this. It is impossible to be lethargic or apathetic when you arch your eyebrows. When your face sags your interest lags. By lifting your eyebrows you animate your face and activate your curiosity.

Lean forward. Think about it. When you are really interested in someone or something, you lean forward in anticipation. You sit on the edge of your seat. By bending forward you are adopting a posture of intrigue, which is the opposite of slumping in your chair and wishing you were anywhere but where you are.

Make a conscious decision to plan your day, slow down, and be present. It is time to take your life back. Busy is not cool. I do not need to have a spastic life in order to be successful.

THOUGHT-PROVOKING QUESTIONS AND ACTION PLANS

1. Do you have a tendency to speed through your days? Do you have so much to do that you find yourself rushing around and constantly feeling behind?

2. Do you have a system for planning your day to move through it proactively rather than reactively? What is that?

3. Do you have a tendency to only half-listen to people when they talk to you? How do you think it makes them feel?

4. How will you counteract the message your children are receiving from the world that being busy is fashionable?

5. As you go through the next week, become conscious of how busy those around you are. Notice that when you ask someone how they are, she will often proudly communicate how spastic her life is. Do you pretend that being busy is cool?

6. Can you make time to relax without feeling guilty? Are you taking your cell phone into the room when you are getting a massage? Do you have to run around cleaning the house because sitting still makes you uncomfortable? Do you allow yourself to feel true peace?

Don't Drop the Ball

*Often people attempt to live their lives backwards. They try
to have more things, or more money, in order to do more of
what they want so they will be happier. The way it actually
works is the reverse. You must first be who you really are, then,
do what you need to do, in order to have what you want.*
—MARGARET YOUNG

A S LEADERS WE can be pulled in many directions. We juggle so many
balls and are often busy taking care of others. We do not always have
appropriate priorities in our lives. *If you don't define your direction, circumstances will.* Each of us needs to make a conscious decision as to who we are
going to be and what we will do with our lives.

Begin the process by becoming very clear about who you really want
to be. Make a list of your current life roles. For example, I am a mother, a
daughter, a grandmother, an employer, a member of the board of directors
for several nonprofit organizations, and a ministry group leader at church.
Making a list of life roles before I create goals forces me to look at what is
taking up my time, money, and attention today.

I think back to how I became involved in each non-optional role (family roles are not optional). I make a list of the reasons that I took on each of these roles. I then try to determine if there at least five good reasons why I am still involved today. If I can't maybe it is no longer a priority.

Going through this process every year forces me to evaluate whether or not I am well rounded. Years ago I did this exercise and most of my roles and goals revolved around my business. As Lord Chesterfield wrote to his son in 1749, "Few people do business well who do nothing else." *I needed a life!* After I looked at each of my current roles and truly reevaluated my involvement, I began creating new goals.

I contemplate what I would like to accomplish in the following categories:

- Spiritual goals (e.g., prayer time, scripture reading, meditating, ministering to others)
- Family goals (e.g., time with children, weekly date with spouse, vacation time)
- Physical goals (e.g., exercise time, drinking plenty of water, eating healthy meals, taking time for a massage regularly)
- Educational goals (e.g., reading personal development and industry information, computer classes, attending conferences)
- Financial goals (e.g., debt free, savings plan, investing, retirement plan contributions)
- Business goals (e.g., 25 percent growth in sales, a specific increase in retention, hiring a new employee)

It is easier for me to create goals in some areas than in others. I find it hardest to create goals in the areas that I tend to neglect. Each day I review my long-term and short-term goals. I try to spend at least one hour a day working toward a long-term goal and eight hours a day working on short-term goals.

Obviously one of the keys to achieve your goals is to realize that you will have to learn to say no at times. A friend taught me that it is easier to stay out of something than it is to get out once you have committed. If I am not sure I will be passionate about spending time in a new role, I probably shouldn't take it on.

In his book *Suzanne's Diary for Nicholas*, James Patterson tells the story of a man who is juggling five balls. The man says, "Understand that work is a rubber ball. If you drop it, it will bounce back. The other four balls—family, health, friends, and integrity—are made of glass. If you drop one of these, it will be irrevocably scuffed, nicked, perhaps even shattered. Once you truly understand the lesson of the five balls, you will have the beginnings of balance in your life."

This lesson became very clear to me several years ago. I had become so preoccupied with my career that I was not giving my daughters the time or attention they deserved. By February of 1999, my oldest daughter and I struggled to see eye to eye. At seventeen, Kristin decided to move out of the house.

By May we had gone for three months of barely speaking. As her high-school graduation approached I was not sure if I would be invited to attend. The graduating seniors provided guests with invitations and the gulf between my daughter and I was so big that she had not given me one. Fortunately, we made amends the day before graduation and I was able to see her accept her diploma.

Five months later Kristin lost a close friend, Crystal. She was not only Kristin's friend but had also worked in our office. The tragedy of Crystal being killed by a drunk driver immediately put our petty arguments into perspective. I had dropped the ball by allowing myself to get out of balance, but thankfully, it had not shattered irreplaceably.

My excessive focus on the business had caused collateral damage. I had everything I had ever wanted yet had never been more miserable. I was fortunate to get a second chance. Kristin and I made amends and are very close today.

It is never too late to do the right thing. Right now, all I can do is the *next* right thing. My goal is keep all six areas of my life in harmony, never again sacrificing one for the other. Of course, it is easy to say and hard to do. It requires frequent gut checks. In order to lead a team in the right direction, I first have to be careful to lead myself in the right direction. Intentionally set priorities and decisively deal with conflicting demands.

I decided to create a visual reminder to maintain balance. I had saved a postcard from every place I had visited in the last five years. I had the postcards framed and put a photo of my daughters and Crystal in the center.

When I become overly anxious, I look at the framed collection and remember what is really most important—my family.

Author John Maxwell makes an important distinction. He says someone who is driven is "impatient, too goal oriented." He feels someone who is passionate "savors the journey." I hope you cherish your relationships and enjoy the journey!

THOUGHT-PROVOKING QUESTIONS AND ACTION PLANS

1. Make a list of your current life roles. Many of these roles are optional. Beside each optional role, make a list of the top five reasons you became involved in that originally. List five reasons why you choose to be involved in that role today.

2. Is your life in balance now? If so, what system do you have in place to make sure you keep all areas of your life in harmony? If not, how can you redistribute your time so that your top priorities are being given adequate attention?

3. Do you have a list of long-term and short-term goals? Do you spend some time every week working toward both?

4. Do you revise your goals at least once a year? Do you have the goals in writing so that you can reflect on them often?

Part 2
UPFRONT ALIGNMENT

Sweat Today or Bleed Tomorrow

I must create a system or be enslaved by another man's.
—WILLIAM BLAKE

YEARS AGO I wanted to find an activity that would keep me both mentally and physically fit. I signed up for six months of Tae Kwon Do and fell in love. Martial arts training helps keep my mind and body in shape, and I have participated for over twenty-five years. An added bonus is the discipline that carries over into other parts of my life.

During one particularly challenging session I noticed a fellow student throwing sloppy kicks. I knew it would not be long before Master Kim would address the situation. My wise instructor used this opportunity to stop the class and provide us with some insight. He said, "Sweat today or bleed tomorrow." I looked at him like he was speaking a foreign language.

He proceeded to explain that the more you train, the more skilled you will become. The more skilled you become, the less likely it is you will be confronted. If you invest in hard, sweaty work today you will have physical self-assurance that drastically decreases the chances that you will be attacked. Training appropriately increases the chance you will defend yourself instinctively if attacked.

The same concept applies in business. As a business owner I must take time to put the foundation of the business in place or it cannot operate smoothly. When consulting with business owners I often hear "I do not have time to create an employee handbook, job descriptions, or an operations manual. I am too busy." Overwhelmed business owners often do not understand. Setting up the foundations of the business prevents confusion and stress. When you create structure in a business you are saving time long term and providing clarity.

The documents I recommend putting in place *upfront* include

- A business plan
- An employee handbook with job descriptions
- A compensation system aligned with business goals
- An operations manual

Do not wait until the time is convenient to create these documents. Face it—there is never a convenient time. Do it *now!*

Originally we tended to spend all of our time selling, selling, and selling. Eventually we became overwhelmed because 100 percent of our effort was geared toward bringing in new customers. We had no documented processes in place to provide structure for employee or customer retention. My lack of organization made it difficult to find time to educate employees in new operations. I did not have processes in place to retain my best customers. Without the upfront alignment, I was losing valuable clients.

We decided to pay the piper and install operating systems. I eventually used the documented processes to train employees so that they, too, would become ingrained in the operation. With consistent, well-defined processes employees are less likely to develop bad habits that may be difficult to break.

Being organized might seem like the "impossible dream" but creating something of lasting value takes time. Establishing the foundation from day one will set clear standards for the operation. You will be pleased when you see employees operate with less duplicated effort and increased productivity. Creating structure reduces the likelihood that damage control will be necessary later.

THOUGHT-PROVOKING QUESTIONS AND ACTION PLANS

1. Do you have a business plan that outlines your operational and financial goals for each quarter?

2. Do you have an employee handbook with job descriptions that provide direction for the business?

3. Is there something you know you should do but you have not been doing it because you have been "too busy"?

4. What is one step you are going to take this week to establish a system that holds everyone accountable for operating more efficiently and productively?

5. If you do have the foundation in place, when is the last time you updated the documents? Are they still providing a strong foundation for the business today?

Begin with the End in Mind

If you don't know where you're going, you'll end up somewhere else.
—Yogi Berra

STEVEN COVEY IS well known for advising us to begin with the end in mind. I am a firm believer in that philosophy. To be successful in business we need to have goals for the next five to ten years but we also need a very clear picture of the end product. What characteristics will my business have on the day I sell it? I need a very specific strategy in mind for my exit. Only by having a clear picture of the end am I able to have a life by design, not default.

When I began my business, I did not have a clear picture of the end goal. It never occurred to me to imagine what the business would look like when it was "finished." It never occurred to me to envision how many employees would be working in the operation or how much it would be worth when I was ready to retire.

As you are building the business you need to visualize the ideal business and a succession plan from day one. As you develop the structure of the business, keep in mind the factors that would increase the value of the business to a potential buyer.

Following are some factors you may want to keep in mind:

- A potential buyer will pay more if the business does not revolve around the current owner. Will it work when you aren't there?
- A potential buyer will pay more for a business that has long-term, stable employees. Are they likely to continue with the operation?
- A potential buyer will pay more for a business that has strong customer retention numbers. Are clear processes in place to consistently provide exceptional service?
- A potential buyer will pay more if the business processes are defined in writing. Could a third party come in and take over where your team left off?
- A potential buyer will pay more if the business has a clearly defined brand with a unique selling proposition. Is there something distinct about your business that will attract future customers?

You need to be able to visualize what the business needs to look like in order to be valuable to an outside buyer. Can you make it happen?

As you make day-to-day business decisions, you need to study possible investments into the business. Is the investment that you are contemplating moving you closer to achieving the established short-term and long-term business and personal goals?

You also need a clear picture of what is required for you to have a predictable perpetuation plan. Are there family members who would possibly like to continue the business? What training would they need to be prepared to continue to build the value of the business after you are gone?

Determine the estimated value of your business on a quarterly basis. This will serve as a gut check that allows you to remain focused on the end. Is the business growing as planned? Do you possibly have a depreciating asset and not know it? Do the employees of the organization understand whether or not the business is growing? Do they understand that you cannot afford to play the game for long if the business is becoming less valuable over time?

Begin with a clear picture of the end in mind. Help others within the organization to see the value of living into that vision. You need to operate today like you are going to sell tomorrow. You need to be clear about what you want your business to look like long term.

THOUGHT-PROVOKING QUESTIONS AND ACTION PLANS

1. What can you do to make your business more attractive to future buyers?

2. Have you built relationships with persons who may be interested in purchasing your business someday?

3. Are you considering your employees in light of your eventual transition out of the business? What can you do that will increase the chances they have job security when you transition ownership?

4. Do you have family members who would possibly be interested in ownership when you retire? Have you discussed this possibility with them? If you are considering them as potential buyers, are you beginning to communicate what the conditions would be?

5. Do you have contingency plans in place for transition of ownership in the event you become disabled or die? Have you consulted an attorney regarding this? Have you discussed tax planning and/or estate planning with an attorney? Do you have a will that will make the transition of your business less stressful for your family members?

6. What will your life look like at retirement? Would you like to retain control of your business after you are no longer actively involved?

Don't Stash the Plan

*A clear vision, backed by definite plans, gives you a
tremendous feeling of confidence and personal power.*
—Brian Tracy

O NCE WE HAVE a clear picture of our desired end result, it is time to
decide how we will get there. I confess. I originally thought of a business plan as a stupid paper exercise. Yes, I had one. Each December I would
pull it out, change some of the numbers, and consider the exercise complete
for the next twelve months. I had to label the folder "Business Plan" so I
could locate the paperwork at the end of each year. I was always shocked and
somewhat tickled when we accidentally hit a goal. A business plan simply
was not a functional document for me.

If you create a functional business plan you will make back the price of
this book many times over. A business plan provides everyone with a clear
picture of the end goal as well as an action plan for getting there.

It took several years in business to realize that my original plan of working hard was not the fastest way to the desired goal. Hard work was absolutely necessary, but mapping out a specific route would help us get there

faster. I eventually hauled the business plan out of my drawer and turned it into a living, breathing planning tool. I worked with key staff to map out where we wanted to be in one year, three years, and five years. We then determined a strategy for the fastest way to get there.

It does not have to be a document that looks like it was created by a team of professionals. It does, however, need to be a document that provides clear direction. It also has to contain a measurement system that allows you to determine if you are progressing as planned.

The business plan has two purposes. First, it reminds us of the early years. My business plan includes a "company history"; this story takes us back to the early years with all of its excitement and anxiety. It is a reminder of how unbelievably pathetic our production was in the first year. It is also a reminder that we did not originally have an appropriate emphasis on customer retention.

It brings back memories. Our first office was so bad that we had to bring towels to work when it rained (to keep the rain from coming under the door). We also remember working late into the evening and hearing mice running through the ceiling. Now our business is much more professional. We own our building (which doesn't contain mice).

The second function of the business plan is to provide a clear picture of the desired future. We need to forecast our future. We view the business from three viewpoints—employer, employees, and customers. Our business plan defines clear goals and an action plan.

A strong business plan must not only provide direction; it must also build the confidence level that outsiders have in our organization. If I need to raise capital or approach a bank for a loan, a strong business plan can be a tremendous asset. My business plan should include information on our marketing plans, cash flow projections, and management programs. Also include the exit strategy in your business plan.

In the early years I can remember thinking "I don't need a business plan yet." I was wrong. We would have reduced our stress and grown faster had we created a functional business plan from day one. I recall the confidence that I felt when we completed our first real business plan. It was much more fun playing the game when I had a strategy. Formulate a business plan that is a functional document which actually impacts strategy and tactics.

THOUGHT-PROVOKING QUESTIONS AND ACTION PLANS

1. Do you have a business plan? How often do you refer to it? Is it a living, breathing document or is it strategically filed so you can find it next December?

2. Do you sometimes get lost or take wrong turns with your business or career? It could very well be that your lack of direction is caused by the lack of a clear vision.

3. Does your business plan contain a "company story" that explains the history of your business? New employees need to know not only where the business is going but also how it began. Share the memories of your business with your team to reinforce where you have come from.

4. Do you include key employees in the business planning process? Schedule a retreat to discuss strategies for strengthening the organization. Will employees see a benefit for themselves if they help you create and execute this business plan?

Market by Design, Not by the Seat of Your Pants

In marketing I've seen only one strategy that can't miss—
and that is to market to your best customers first, your
best prospects second and the rest of the world last.
—JOHN ROMERO

I STILL REMEMBER THE day it occurred to me that we really had no marketing plan. Our strategy was basically to act upon random ideas as they
came up. Our marketing program was sporadic events—not intentionally
scheduled programs. It occurred to me that real businesses didn't just show
up and market in a haphazard fashion. A marketing plan should naturally
be part of a strong business plan.

As John Romero so eloquently put it, "Market to your best customers
first." How do we determine who our best customers are? Success in business requires that we continually look at the dynamics of the consumer, as
their demographics and their priorities change.

We studied our most profitable customers to see what characteristics they have in common. Were they brought to us through a particular source? Do they purchase a particular product? Which clients are most likely to refer others? What was the typical age of our best customers? How do they want to buy our products?

How often does our ideal customer want to be contacted? Does he become more profitable if we do business over the phone, in person, or online? We had to shift our thinking from selling products to identifying ideal prospects. After determining the characteristics and buying habits of the ideal customer, we had to become clear on what we could do to attract that person to our organization. What does our brand need to represent in order to meet the ideal prospect's needs?

Unfortunately, if I cannot articulate clearly why a prospect should do business with us, what are the odds that the employees can? If the employees cannot articulate clearly why a prospect should do business with us, what are the odds that the customers see us as unique? If the customers cannot understand what distinguishes us from the competition, what are the odds they will send a referral? *Zero.*

We need to be able to clearly articulate what makes us unique. We need to have the reasons documented (we call our document Top 10 Reasons to do Business with Pinnacle Insurance).

After we have studied our best customers and defined our uniqueness, our second emphasis has to be on new prospects. Once we have a clear picture of what our best customers look like, we are better prepared to go after them. Where do they shop? What appeals to them? How can we distinguish our business to attract this ideal consumer?

We designed an annual marketing program and created a calendar to document exactly what our monthly processes would be. They included selling additional products and increasing retention of existing customers. In January we had a plan for how we would market throughout the entire year—both internally and externally.

Some business owners are of the mentality that any customer is a good customer. I am of the opinion that I am better off without some clients. Why not design processes that are more likely to attract the ideal client? We don't turn away customers that don't meet the ideal criteria, but they represent a small percentage of our business.

We work to attract a certain niche and become their "go-to" resource within the market. The more specifically we identify our niche, the more specific we can be with advertising and marketing. This clarity makes obtaining referrals easier. As you become known as the expert within your industry, referrals are earned.

We also studied our current income stream. We became very aware of which months provide the biggest challenges economically. Once we were clear on which months had the least income, we could concentrate specifically on additional marketing and advertising to drive in business then.

We maintain several types of marketing projects. Having diverse marketing programs reduces the negative effects if any one process has to be discontinued. Never put all of your eggs in one basket.

Marketing entails the activities designed to attract buyers to a business. Some approaches of a marketing plan can include

- Referral marketing—encouraging proactive word of mouth from customers, vendors, related businesses, etc.
- Public relations—managing the image of the business in the community, being newsworthy and creating media around your business
- Trade shows—showcasing products in an industry-specific setting
- Event marketing—contemplating events in the community that tie well to your mission
- Direct marketing—targeting specific customers directly by mail
- Internet marketing—using electronic means to market to prospects
- Personal sales—closing deals based on the art of persuasion
- Advertising—paying for a persuasive message

Be creative and be flexible. Do not become so attached to your plan that you can't adapt if market conditions change or a new opportunity arises. Write the plan in pencil—figuratively.

Design your plan, then track new customers to see which marketing and advertising programs draw in the best customers. Create a marketing program that proactively attracts the ideal customer.

THOUGHT-PROVOKING QUESTIONS AND ACTION PLANS

1. Does your business have a marketing plan or is marketing done by the seat of your pants?

2. If you have a marketing plan, does it include specific promotional campaigns tied to relevant events?

3. Has your business identified a target customer? If so, what are the characteristics of that person?

4. Does your marketing program identify ways to sell and retain your existing customers in addition to attracting new ones?

5. What are the demographics of your best prospects? How are you more likely to attract them than your competition?

6. What products are most likely to attract your ideal prospect? What will your profit margin be on this product?

7. What is your marketing budget? How will you allocate these funds?

Take the Personal Out of It

Intellectuals solve problems; geniuses prevent them.
—ALBERT EINSTEIN

I CAN RECALL TELLING my parents, "That's not fair," as a child. I certainly heard it a few times as a parent. There were times that I heard "That's not fair" from employees. Now I understand how miserable I made my mother.

In the business world there are times when I am forced to make personnel decisions. No matter how fair I try to be, it is impossible to make everyone happy. I can, however, prevent most issues by having an employee handbook to address situations that could cause hard feelings.

For example, an employee asked for a day off to attend a relative's funeral. Of course, that was not an issue. Two months later another employee had a relative die in another state. One day off would not allow her to get to the funeral and back. I struggled with what was fair. You guessed it. I despise conflict. I needed a system that allowed me to run the business with structure and stability.

Employees all have personal lives. They have children who want them to attend school functions, family members who have medical appointments, personal errands that can be run only during business hours. If you decide on a case-by-case basis how to handle each situation, you will drive yourself crazy. There will also be situations where one person feels someone else is getting special treatment.

Most conflict can be avoided by creating an employee handbook. This document reduces stress for everyone involved by defining most possible scenarios with forethought instead of making decisions in the heat of the moment. An employee handbook will radically reduce the odds of chaos. It should be constructed prior to hiring the first employee. This document reduces the chances that there will be a misunderstanding or a mismatch between job and applicant.

We eventually put together an employee handbook from scratch. Originally, it was only ten pages. It grew over time as new issues arose. We created impartial guidelines to provide clarity and reduce the "That's not fair" complaint.

I cannot tell you what a godsend this handbook has been! Each time a sensitive situation comes up, instead of my office manager or me having to make a subjective decision, we refer to the handbook. This document has taken the personal out of personnel issues by having them spelled out in writing.

Designing an employee handbook can be a monumental task but it does not have to be. Through the Internet or an attorney you can obtain an inexpensive template that can make it easy.

(Note: Be sure to get legal advice regarding state and federal laws before using this or any other employee handbook to make sure you are in accordance with regulations.)

After an employee handbook is written, provide a copy to each employee. Have each employee sign an acknowledgement of receipt.

Life is not always scripted. Of course, there are times when it is necessary to have exceptions to the rules. It is crucial that I use common sense regarding my business. I wouldn't want to work for someone who took "by the book" to an extreme. For example, if I have a rule that says employees must be licensed within three months and a new employee has a death in the immediate family during that time, I may choose to make an exception. Exceptions, however, are few and far between.

An employee handbook will reduce the possibility of disputes and litigation with employees. If I choose to enforce some rules but not all of them, then I risk potential lawsuits for discrimination. The document that was used to create clarity could be used against me in court.

Don't include a rule that you are not willing to enforce. I consulted with a business owner several years ago who was struggling with a personnel issue. My first question was "Do you have an employee handbook?" He quickly answered affirmatively.

Next I asked, "Is this situation addressed in the handbook?" Again he proudly nodded affirmatively. The business owner had taken the personal out of this situation. He had taken the right steps by creating and communicating the rules. Unfortunately he had put a rule in his employee handbook that he was unwilling to enforce. He had confused and frustrated employees. The employee who was not abiding by the rules was getting the message that some rules were serious and some were not. The other employees were frustrated because they perceived preferential treatment.

Create it, communicate it, and enforce it. You will have set expectations and prevented problems. Creating an employee handbook that sets clear expectations makes management easier.

THOUGHT-PROVOKING QUESTIONS AND ACTION PLANS

1. Do you have an employee handbook? If so, when was it created and when was the last time you updated it?

2. What types of guidelines are in your employee handbook? What was a delicate situation you were able to resolve fairly by referring to your handbook?

3. Have you ever had an employee claim "that's not fair"? How did you handle that situation?

4. When you encounter a new situation regarding employee privileges, do you make it a practice to amend the employee handbook to include that situation? If not, how are you going to make that standard operating procedure?

5. Think back to personnel problems you have had in the past. Could any of those issues have been prevented if you had addressed them in your employee handbook?

Stay in the Helicopter

You think America is the biggest place on Earth, but it's not. The view from Mir put everything in perspective.
—Shannon Lucid

AS AN ASTRONAUT, Shannon Lucid was able to spend time on the Mir space station seeing the "big picture." How often do we get so focused on our own little world that we lose sight of the bigger picture? Is it possible we do not see the forest for the trees?

I had an opportunity to fly over the Grand Canyon in a helicopter. To this day I remember swooping down over the rim and following the mighty Colorado River as it twisted through the rocky canyon walls. It was a magnificent experience. The helicopter eventually landed inside the canyon. I was shocked at the difference in the view from the air versus on the ground. From the ground, everything looked dry and bleak. From the sky, the canyon was quite colorful. Instead of being brown, the canyon walls were a mixture of pink, gray, tan, and purple. It was amazingly beautiful and a distinctively different view. Hmmm. Same place, different perspective.

I decided to look at my business "from a helicopter." We can get so buried in the day-to-day work that we miss some of the landscape. We get so caught up in just staying caught up that we become robotic. We stop evaluating whether or not we are still headed in the right direction as we keep doing things the way we have always done them.

We decided to evaluate every office task with fresh eyes. We were shocked at the wasted effort we discovered and amazed at how much time and money we were spending on non-income-producing activities.

For instance, we were paying someone to spend three hours a day filing. Filing does not generate income and we found a way to keep paperwork according to transaction date—eliminating the need for customer files. Another example was my almost daily drive to the post office. We leased a postage machine and stopped the ritual of leaving the office every afternoon. The non-income-producing activities were many. Some could be avoided; some could not. Not only did we save the money that was being spent on that task but employees were now free to spend those hours on income-producing activities. We were not just saving money—we were generating money!

Remember—activity is not the same as accomplishment. We need to reevaluate the correlation between each activity and the bottom-line results we are attempting to achieve. There is a correlation between activity and results.

A friend of mine calls this "The Waitress Rule." She said on her first day as a waitress, the savvy restaurant owner gave her advice she still remembers and uses today. He told her, "I have one word for you. Consolidate. Never do one thing when you can do three."

He explained, "If you make a trip to the kitchen to pick up an order, always ask yourself, 'What else can I get while I am here?' Maybe you can grab fresh cream for Table 4 while you deliver the food to Table 5."

My friend told me, "That was my training ground for multitasking. We never made an empty trip." Her perspective reminded me to continuously reevaluate our efficiencies.

Who knows? A different vantage point might help streamline and consolidate systems so less time and money is wasted. Spend some time in the helicopter without losing touch with the day-to-day operation. Envision a holistic perspective of the business which leads the strategy of the day-to-day operations.

THOUGHT-PROVOKING QUESTIONS AND ACTION PLANS

1. Are you so focused on daily routine that you no longer see the big picture? How are you going to get a different perspective on your business? Are there any optional processes in your organization that are not generating income? How could those be eliminated or transformed to free up people to engage in higher-return activities?

2. Can you consolidate tasks so you are not making unnecessary trips? Brainstorm with your staff on how you can use "The Waitress Rule" to do more than one thing at a time.

3. Is your business utilizing modern technology to increase operational efficiency?

4. Ask a friend or business associate to stand at the front door of your business. What do they see that creates a positive or a negative impression of your business? Are there stacks of files or messages? Does the physical appearance of your business instill confidence or damage the brand image?

Hitting the Wall

I HAVE HIT THE wall as a runner. A beautiful run that seemed to come fairly easy turns painful and I begin to wonder if I can take another step. I have completely depleted my physical resources. My body gives up and my spirit is temporarily squelched.

I have also hit the wall as a writer. I seem to be in the groove as I write an article, then bam, all of the sudden my brain is completely blank.

The same phenomenon happens in business. There are times when our business seems to be running on all cylinders, then all of the sudden we have hit the not-so-imaginary wall.

I know what it feels like to work really hard and feel like the business is not progressing. The business seems to have grown to its maximum capacity, and no matter how hard everyone works, the value of the business is not growing.

There are two ways to tackle hitting the wall. Prevent it or deal with it. Your ability to overcome the collapse of momentum is determined more by willpower than anything else. Of course, we would always like to avoid hitting the wall. Whether I am working to prevent or doing damage control on stalled progress, I need to do a few gut checks.

Common conditions include the following:

- Hire ahead of the curve. I have found that most businesses that hit the wall are understaffed. They are unable to grow because they do not have an adequate number of people to adequately serve existing customers while simultaneously bringing in new prospects. It took me a while to understand that the minute I mentally put a lid on the number of employees I would have, I was limiting my potential for growth of the business. When I chose to stop hiring employees, I chose to eventually limit our growth.

- Consistently review the basics. Review the basic processes to make sure they are all still taking place. Is there a need to review basic product knowledge or sales skills? Are the processes that you had in place when you were making significant gains still in place? Are they still being carried out in the same way?

- Think big. We outgrew our first business location within two years. The business had grown so fast that we no longer fit in the physical location we were operating from. Do you need to think bigger?

- Did you get greedy? We live in a materialistic country that defines success by possession of assets. Business owners can get greedy with profits and reduce the business's ability to grow. Am I investing enough in the business to allow for the progress that we need?

- Review consumer preferences. Did something in the market or consumer preferences change? Are competitors pursuing the ideal consumer in a way that is providing them an advantage? Maybe I am still forcing customers to buy in person when they prefer to do business online? Study the consumer and the competition.

- Back away from the situation. At times, it is beneficial to take some time off. It may be beneficial for the team to take a day off and do a SWOT analysis (strengths, weaknesses, opportunities, and threats).

Difficulties are inevitable in life and in business. These challenges can actually bring a team closer together as you work together on a solution. You must build confidence in your ability to assess and realign if momentum is lost.

THOUGHT-PROVOKING QUESTIONS AND ACTION PLANS

1. Have you ever been part of a business that hit the wall? What was it like for employees to be working as hard as they could but to feel they were not making any progress?

2. Do you have a measurable system for knowing when to hire new people? Do you have the space, financial resources, and staff necessary to reach the corporate goals?

3. Have you put a limit on how many employees you think could work for you? What is it? Are you comfortable with your decision to ultimately limit your potential growth?

4. Look at your current office. Is its physical size keeping you from having room to grow?

5. Does your team need to take some time off to reevaluate your strategic plan? Are you ready to take an objective look at your strengths, weaknesses, opportunities, and threats?

6. Are you getting greedy? Are you stunting the business's potential by investing less than is needed?

The Secret Is—
There Is No Secret

*I'd gone through life believing in the strengths and com-
petence of others; never in my own. Now, dazzled, I
discovered that my capacities were real. It was like finding a fortune in the lining of an old coat.*

—JOAN MILLS

EARLY IN MY career I spent a lot of time visiting successful business
owners to learn their secrets of success. I also had a voracious appetite
for business books. I knew that many successful leaders had put their secrets
to success in writing. Exactly one year after I opened my business I was
invited to a two-day seminar in Houston, Texas. The purpose of the program
was to increase product knowledge.

I was excited about attending this meeting because I was going to meet
a woman who was my hero, Joanne Harris. Joanne began her business at

almost the exact same time I did, but her business was selling twice as much as mine. Boy, I had her on a pedestal.

I could not wait to meet her. I thought, *I will get to know this really successful business owner and learn her secret.* At that time in my life, I perceived the most successful persons to possess some type of magic.

Guess what I discovered? Joanne had fewer employees, typical marketing programs, and was living in a town a fraction of the size of mine. The magic bubble burst. There was no magic.

What I learned in May 1995 was to stop looking for secrets. They simply do not exist. I am the one who is responsible for my success or failure. *Searching for a magic formula gave me an excuse not to succeed.* Feeling that others had some special process or exceptional market conditions gave me permission to remain mediocre.

Once I knew there was no secret, I became solely responsible for my own success or failure. If I was not doing exceptionally well, there was no one to blame but myself.

When I peeled away the veneer of the magic formula, instead of perceiving Joanne as being more competent I realized I held the key to my success. We had a dramatic and immediate increase of momentum with this realization.

I assure you this book will provide insights and some new perspectives—however, there are no shortcuts. The magic formula for success is being willing to work hard toward a clearly defined goal while refusing to be held back by fictitious limitations or excuses.

After I read all of the wonderful books to improve my business and met all of the right people to provide insight, I had to get to work.

The good news is there is no magic formula and seldom is there a particular process that will radically propel you to success. You don't have to be exceptionally smart or work twenty-four hours a day. The secret is—there aren't any secrets. We must accept and understand that people at the top do not have a magic formula.

THOUGHT-PROVOKING QUESTIONS AND ACTION PLANS

1. Are you looking for a magic formula? Are you hoping there is a secret that can catapult you to success?

2. What do you believe is impossible? Is it possible that you are holding yourself back by believing you are limited in some way?

3. Is there a reason (excuse) you give yourself for not performing as well as other business owners? Is your team content with mediocre performance?

4. What is one specific thing you are going to do differently in order to perform up to your potential? How are you going to take personal responsibility for your own success?

5. Do you spend all of your time reading books trying to learn the secret instead of implementing things you have already learned?

6. Who do you have on a pedestal? How can you get close enough to that person to determine what they are truly like? When will you realize that you are capable of being as competent as your hero?

Written Goals Become Reality

Take a minute: look at your goals, look at your
performance, see if your behavior matches your goals.
—KENNETH BLANCHARD, PH.D., SPENCER JOHNSON, M.D.

MY YOUNGEST DAUGHTER, Kara's, first endeavor at sales was at the age of ten. Her school was selling cookies to raise money for new playground equipment. Kara called me at work and informed me that she wanted to be the number-one salesperson so that she would win a new bicycle. She asked if she could begin selling immediately. I hated to squelch her enthusiasm so I told her she could sell on the three streets in our neighborhood but only if she could find a friend willing to tag along.

An hour later Kara called again, clearly exasperated. I asked, "Honey, what's wrong?" She complained, "Jackie would only walk door to door with me for two streets. She said she was tired." She continued with "I informed her—I have a goal of selling thirty boxes today and I am not stopping until I do."

I thought I was going to die laughing. I shouldn't have been so tickled since she was upset. I thought it was completely bizarre that this ten-year-old child was articulating her goals with such clarity. I doubt very seriously that I knew what a goal was when I was ten! She could see the bicycle in her mind and had determined what it would take to get it.

Surprisingly Kara did not win the bicycle—she did, however, teach me a lesson. A clear mental picture of her dream and determination to be the best provided tremendous motivation. She knew what she wanted and had an action plan established.

Prior to opening my business I attended a sales training program. At the end of the program each participant was videotaped while simulating a sales presentation. We watched the videos afterward and waited to be critiqued. I can only describe the person that critiqued my video as Ms. Sourpuss.

Unfortunately I was the first victim. She watched my video and proceeded to tear me apart. The first words out of her mouth were "You will never make it in business. You are too professional. No one will buy from you." Too professional?! What the heck did that mean?!

At home that night, I thought about her comment—actually I stewed. I eventually realized that I had a choice. I could either allow her negativity to determine my future, or I could move forward with even greater resolve. I was not going to allow her to declare me incapable. I was going to succeed!

Back in my new office I looked around, wondering what I could do to remind myself not to be "too professional." Her words seemed to continually ring in my head. A brilliant solution finally occurred to me. I decided to paint my office. I chose a feminine pink color that became a reminder that I didn't need to be too professional with customers. It was my rebellious "I'll show you!" declaration. I would surround myself with a visible reminder that success was within my control; it was my choice.

I created very specific sales goals for the remainder of the year. I decided to reward myself with a trip to San Juan, Puerto Rico, if I reached the goal.

Every morning I wrote, "I am lying on the beaches of San Juan." In addition, I wrote an affirmation that became my mantra, "Winners are those who make a habit of doing what others feel uncomfortable doing." I woke up every day vowing to prove to my nemesis that I would succeed despite her prediction. I literally visualized myself frolicking in the ocean, sunbathing on the beach, and basking in the warm, tropical sun. I found a photo of the San Juan beach and taped it to my computer.

Guess what? We made our sales goals. We had clearly begun with the end in mind. When I arrived in San Juan, I checked into the hotel, changed clothes, and walked straight to the beach. I sat down and cried. I felt a mixture of emotions. I had lived this moment every day for seven months. My affirmation and visualization had made this a goal, not just a dream. I was proud, relieved, exhausted, and thrilled all at the same time.

I learned the power of identifying a clear goal and writing it down every day. The direction of our business was clear. We analyzed every process to determine whether or not the process was moving us closer to the goal. Writing it down once would not have been adequate for me. The daily exercise was a crucial factor in my success.

Written goals become reality. It is that simple.

I realized the disapproving instructor had actually done me a favor. By telling me I was doomed, she had made me even more determined to succeed.

Designing your specific individual goals is foundational to running a strong business and being a well-rounded person. It is not uncommon for the practice of goal setting to stir up negative emotions. We have all set goals and not achieved them. Putting goals in writing and creating visual reminders of them increases the chance of success.

I had to decide to create goals without guilt. Instead of allowing goals to intimidate me or feeling guilty when I did not meet a deadline, I expended my energy on celebrating the goals that I did manage to achieve. I decided that having goals would be a positive inspiration in my life, not a burden.

We must acknowledge that other people will not always believe in our dreams. Who cares! What matters is that we have well-rounded goals that create passion in us and in those closest to us.

Today I focus on my calendar. I journal every day so I do not forget the lessons I have learned. I review my business and personal goals every morning so they are fresh in my mind. I visualize myself reaping the reward of persevering and accomplishing what I have set out to do.

Chances are, what you have vividly imagined will happen as you have imagined it. Enjoy passionately working toward your goals as you watch them become reality. Write affirmations and visualize them to provide momentum and create enthusiasm. Define your personal and business goals in writing.

THOUGHT-PROVOKING QUESTIONS AND ACTION PLANS

1. What is a specific, measurable goal you could get excited about pursuing? Choose a big dream that you can passionately work toward. Describe that goal in vivid detail as you see it in your mind. Design a feasible, meaningful reward for achieving the goal. How will you make this goal tangible and visual?

2. What system will you use to write down and review goals daily? If your goal is to give up something, share it with everyone so they will help hold you accountable (e.g., giving up smoking, giving up drinking sodas). Share your goals of achievement (e.g., doubling your income this year) with only your most supportive friends.

3. Have you ever had a naysayer predict that you would fail or that you were incapable of achieving something? Did you let that person intimidate you into giving up or did their prediction inspire you to try harder?

4. Have you ever achieved a major goal? Did you feel tremendous pride at your accomplishment? Was there somewhat of a void after that major goal was accomplished? Did you move on to other goals naturally?

5. Here is an interesting fact. A study supposedly conducted by Yale University indicated that the 3 percent of graduating seniors who had written goals had accumulated more personal financial wealth than the other 97 percent of the class combined. (But an article published in the magazine *Fast Company* in 1996 exposed that this "study" never actually took place. The article can be viewed at http://pf.fastcompany.com/magazine/06/cdu.html.) OK, so this premise may not be accurate. *Who cares!* It's still fascinating. Written goals work!

Whose Goals Are They?

*Whether or not we support a decision depends a
lot on whether it's being done to us or by us.*
—SAM HORN

CHRISTMAS HOLIDAYS HAVE tremendous meaning in our family. Christmas morning was the coolest. It was not necessarily the gifts we received; the family time was special. One particular Christmas stands out. I was twelve years old, my sister Cyndi was ten, and my little brother Greg was just three.

Cyndi and I always stayed up late discussing what was to come, and we woke up early in anticipation of the fun. We were typically awake around 5:00 a.m. Our parents had only one rule regarding Christmas morning. We had to get the coffee ready before we could attempt to get everyone out of bed.

This particular holiday Cyndi and I woke up, started the coffee, and ran to roust our parents out of bed. Unfortunately that year, our parents put a new rule into play. We were informed we could not open presents until Greg got out of bed.

At first we thought this was a fairly minor obstacle. Cyndi and I bounded into Greg's room. He was fast asleep. We bounced up and down on his twin bed. I can still see the red-and-blue basketball light fixture overhead. We announced merrily, "Greg, time to get up. It's Christmas!"

Greg did not stir. I was shocked. Nothing we said made a dent in his semi-comatose state. In our most enthusiastic voice we proclaimed again, *"It's Christmas!"*

Nothing. Nada. He kept snuggling back under the covers. Eventually we had the bright idea, "Let's start unloading his Christmas stocking." Surely seeing what Santa had brought would force his curiosity to kick in. We dumped the contents of his stocking on the floor next to his bed. We began our oohs and aahs as we described in detail each of the contents. He still refused to open his eyes.

It seemed to take us an eternity to get Greg moving. No matter how we tried to prioritize his day, he refused to budge. I can remember my young mind being completely shocked that I did not have the ability to convince him to "listen to reason." It was the year that I realized not everyone in the world had the same priorities as me. Imagine that!

I had the same epiphany with my business years later. I had set some ambitious goals for the business and worked hard to get the team enthusiastic about meeting them. Hardly a day went by that I did not check on sales and encourage the team.

One day, an employee reached her wits' end. She told me point blank, "You're acting like we should treat this business like it's ours. I am not going to treat this business like it's my own. It's not."

I mentally reverted back to my twelve-year-old self. I was shocked that she was out of sync with my plans. She should be as excited about these goals as I was. My initial reaction was "Why *aren't* you committed to achieving these goals?"

Reality check.

I had created the business goals and dumped them on my employees. No wonder they were not excited about achieving them. They had nothing to do with designing them. They were my goals, not their goals. Those goals had been given *to* them, not created *by* them.

Now we work on creating goals as a team. We have an annual planning retreat to work together on crafting our direction. Once we agree upon goals that are meaningful and attainable, we get to work. This time everyone is on board.

By the way, that employee who called me on my autocratic leadership style was with me when we opened the business and is still with me today. I continue to thank her for this wake-up call and many others. Goals that are designed by the entire team are pursued by the entire team.

THOUGHT-PROVOKING QUESTIONS AND ACTION PLANS

1. Who designs the goals that your business is currently working toward?

2. Are your employees committed to the organizational goals? Are all employees at every level aware of the organizational goals?

3. Have you ever taken your team off-site for a business planning retreat?

4. Does your business have regular checkpoint meetings to make sure you stay focused on the goals?

Measure All Your
Critical Variables

Success has always been easy to measure. It is the distance
between one's origins and one's final achievement.
—Michael Korda

FOR THE FIRST several years in business we measured one thing—
sales. We were religious about reviewing our sales results daily.
We kept a dry-erase board with the monthly production in a highly visible place. Each individual kept a report on his desk of his individual
production for the month to provide focus.

A successful business owner in casual conversation mentioned, "Wait
until you have been in business for a few years. One day you will have 3,000
accounts and be losing 300 a year. Then you will work hard all day long just
to break even."

Talk about a Homer moment! I went into shock. I knew that an average
business in my industry had 90 percent retention. I had never thought about

the cold hard fact that if I had 3,000 clients, that meant I would be losing 300 of them a year. I felt as I had been verbally slapped.

I went back to my business and looked at our retention number for the first time. It was below the industry average. By measuring sales and only sales, I was leaving a lot of money on the table. Yes, I had created a "sales machine," but I realized (thankfully, not too late) that I was not playing the right game. A small increase in retention drastically increases the value of the business, whereas a small increase in production is barely seen.

Now I understand that sales are important, but growth is *everything*. If your business is not growing, you are working really hard to break even. Remember that retention keeps you in contention.

I assume the gentleman that created this aha moment was frustrated because he had hit the wall. He was working hard but was no longer seeing the value of his business grow substantially. His comment reinforced what I knew—it would become more and more difficult to increase the business value as it grew. As a new business owner, I could easily grow by focusing on sales. But in order to grow long term, I would also have to have a strong plan in place to maintain customer retention.

We decided it was time to measure something besides sales. We sat down and determined what measurable characteristics we needed to keep an eye on. Of course, the characteristics were determined by the factors that would increase the value of the business long term.

We created a new measurement system. We had to determine what we could quantifiably measure that would be an accurate indicator of success. We decided our measurements would be based on two criteria:

1. An item that would increase cash flow to the business

2. A characteristic that would indicate whether or not we were moving toward our long-term goal of increased business value

We set specific individual and team goals for the categories that are aggressive but not out of reach. We began looking at those trends weekly. We finally had a truer, more accurate measure of whether or not we were progressing.

I have worked with business owners in the past who doubled their production without changing one process by being specific in measuring key variables. Having a clear picture of exactly how the business is trending on critical variables can inspire the team.

Collecting objective evidence of your business performance allows you to accurately evaluate what is working. Measure key variables and show everyone the numbers. A strong measurement system will indicate how the team is progressing toward the predetermined goals.

THOUGHT-PROVOKING QUESTIONS AND ACTION PLANS

1. Do you collect statistical data on the different aspects of your business performance so you know if you are progressing or regressing? What are those measurable processes and how do they operate?

2. What was an important trend you caught—either a good trend on which you were able to capitalize or a bad trend you were able to correct?

3. If you do not currently have criteria in place to assess your business performance in these areas, how are you going to initiate a program?

4. If you measure critical variables, do you share them with everyone? Do your part-time and full-time employees understand how their job duties impact the critical variables?

5. Is your business appropriately focused on sales and customer retention? Do you have a tendency to lose balance by taking focus off one or the other?

Four Good Quarters Make One Great Year

My parents always told me I wouldn't amount to anything because I procrastinated so much. I told 'em, Just you wait.

—Judy Tenuta

O UR TEAM IS very competitive. This mentality can make the last few months of the year feel like a pressure cooker as we stress to make the final numbers. The end of the year is always a push to do the last-minute things necessary to make sure we achieved our annual goals. There is an increase in pressure in the fourth quarter to play catch-up in the areas where we are not on pace. I had an employee who teasingly threatened to take all of her vacation in December each year to avoid the year-end stress.

What is often even more difficult is starting each new year. Every new fiscal year provides the challenge of starting over again at *zero*. In January comes the depressing realization that what we had done the prior year was great, but it is time to start over. Those zeros made us feel like zeros. We had climbed the mountain, then fallen to the bottom, and now we had to start climbing the mountain all over again.

In 1996 I met a business owner who had solved this dilemma. I spent the day studying his operation and picked up lots of tips to utilize in my own business. At the end of the day I came straight out and asked him, "What do you think makes your operation exceptional?" Without hesitation he responded, "We have four good quarters."

He went on to say, "I know what you do. You work hard all year long. Then in November and December you panic because there are areas in which you are lagging. I don't play that game. I set my annual goals in January. In March we check to see if we are on pace. If we need to make adjustments, we make them immediately. We do the same thing in June and September. We enjoy the holidays at the end of the year." I was struck by his words. I'd *never* enjoyed the holidays.

We found that by checking the status of annual goals every three months, only minor adjustments were needed at the end of the year. The status checks identified deficiencies early instead of waiting until the last minute.

His insight helped me realize that just having measurements was not enough. If we were not on pace for our annual goals, we could not afford to procrastinate. The longer we waited, the more difficult corrections became.

Now our goal is to have four good quarters. December is just another month. We no longer panic at the end of the year and therefore are less depressed at the beginning of the year. We chose a mentality to adapt behavior quickly when our organization was not on pace to meet goals.

THOUGHT-PROVOKING QUESTIONS AND ACTION PLANS

1. How often do you check your progress toward your annual requirements and goals? If you wait until late in the year to find out how you are doing, how does that impact your team's morale and productivity?

2. Is there an area of your business where you are guilty of procrastination? What particular task do you tend to put off because you do not like doing it?

3. What system could you set up to help you keep current on your activities? When will the checkpoints be?

4. Do your employees get frustrated with your year-end anxiety? How can you create enthusiasm throughout the year to achieve the goals?

The Man Who Chases Two Rabbits Catches None

Beware of dissipating your powers; strive constantly to concentrate them.
—Goethe

A s MENTIONED EARLIER, I love Tae Kwon Do. After six months of training, I mentioned to my Korean master that I was considering studying a different style of martial arts. I explained to him that I enjoyed Tae Kwon Do but I thought it would be interesting to take some judo classes too. My instructor's face showed his disappointment as he simply said, "The man who chases two rabbits catches none." He then turned and walked away without any explanation.

My initial response was shock. He was clearly offended; I did not understand why. What was this about rabbits?! I was talking about judo. After much thought, I eventually realized what he was trying to say.

If I tried to learn more than one martial art at a time, I would not master either of them. After twenty-five years practicing Tae Kwon Do, I understand how naïve I was. I was ready to move to something else with the assumption that I knew everything there was to know after a mere six months. He must have thought I had lost my mind.

I try to keep this principle in mind in the business world. I am an idea person. My mind is like a popcorn machine, constantly conjuring up new, better, faster, and more profitable ways of doing things. I also enjoy attending conferences and getting ideas for personal and business development. Our business is extremely successful because of our commitment to continual learning. Creative people create things. I have to discipline myself not to pursue every idea that pops into my head.

I have to multitask at times in order to get everything done. I do, however, need to be careful with the compulsion to race off after the next new thing just because it sounds enticing or looks promising. I also face a danger of chasing too many rabbits when I try to do everything in the business myself. I learned to delegate or outsource the activities that I do not enjoy or don't do well.

Accounting made me miserable, so I let a bookkeeper do it. It was inexpensive to outsource this task. I stayed focused on the activities that provided the biggest return on my investment of my time. I focused on the activities that energized me.

On those occasions when an idea occurs to me and I am tempted to chase it, I have to slow down and think it through. Would this activity diffuse my energy and cause the business to become less effective? Would it be wiser to concentrate my efforts and focus on one specific activity instead of chasing rabbits? Focus on specific activities that create success and delegate, outsource, or eliminate all else.

THOUGHT-PROVOKING QUESTIONS AND ACTION PLANS

1. Do you occasionally chase rabbits by agreeing to take on responsibility that either is not within your strengths or is more than you can handle?

2. Do you like to start projects but not always finish them? Do you recall a specific time when you stuck with a project to the end and felt a great sense of accomplishment?

3. Would your focus be improved if you wrote your goals down and found an accountability partner to work with? What criteria are you going to use to make sure a decision to pursue a new activity is wise, not rash?

4. What activities in your job are draining you? Do you have a person in your operation who could take on those tasks or should you hire an outsider to take them off your plate?

You Are in It for the Money

Have you ever noticed that those people whom you see jogging day
after day are the ones who seem not to need to jog? But that's why
they are fit. Those who are wealthy work at staying financially fit.
But those who are not financially fit do little to change their status.
—THOMAS J. STANLEY AND WILLIAM D. DANKO

A WARDS AND ADMIRATION are great but they don't pay the bills. Zig
Ziglar has said, "Money isn't everything but it's reasonably close to
oxygen." Amen.

A healthy cash flow and a healthy emergency fund are required to stay
in business long term. In addition, business owners must remain focused
on whether or not the overall value of the business is increasing over time.
Financial management is not always easy or fun but it is crucial.

My distaste for finances began when I was eight years old. My mother
and I were shopping. We eventually headed to the cash register. The clerk
tried to process my mother's credit card repeatedly to no avail. She finally
looked up and said, "Ma'am, there is a problem with your card. I need you to

follow me." The clerk walked to the back of the store. My mother and I followed obediently. Initially the situation did not bother me at all. It seemed to be a minor inconvenience, somewhat of an adventure. Quickly, however, everything changed. I realized my mother was horribly embarrassed and I decided maybe this was a big deal. I now know that my mother was horrified because she was so responsible and being perceived as financially irresponsible was unacceptable. My mother was informed that her current payment was past due. She made the payment immediately and we went on our way.

The situation probably did not upset my mother for long. I, on the other hand, was scarred. For years I did not feel comfortable even walking into that store, and to this day, have never used a credit card there. Talk about silly scars.

As an adult I realized that I really disliked finances because of the childhood incident. I decided the easiest way to eliminate the fear of financial concerns was to become an expert on finances. Becoming knowledgeable on the topic would take some of the pain and mystique out of it.

I went to the bookstore and bought every book imaginable on becoming a millionaire. I wasn't really concerned about becoming rich but I was extremely determined to always feel financially secure.

Thomas Stanley and William Danko's book *The Millionaire Next Door* changed my perspective on money and wealth. The text explains that wealth is described by the average American as "having an abundance of material possessions." Stanley and Danko defined the wealthy as those people who "get much more pleasure from owning substantial amounts of appreciable assets than from displaying a high-consumption lifestyle."

I had bought into the "American dream." I admired people who appeared to have everything their heart desired. I was not wealthy but was purchasing a new car every two years. I almost subconsciously used this as a declaration that I was successful.

I made a conscious decision not to keep up with the Joneses. I eventually realized it was much more fun to build wealth than spend money. When I catch myself becoming materialistic, I stop in my tracks. I try to remember that often the person that drives an insanely expensive car is a "decoy" rich person. They may have nothing in the bank.

If you want to be successful in business, study money. Dave Ramsey, Robert Kiyosaki, and Thomas Stanley are among my favorite authors. I do not study money to become rich but to better understand what habits and behaviors create financial security. I don't need the material stuff, but I love life that doesn't include financial stress.

After gaining the knowledge of what it takes to achieve financial success, I applied the concepts to my business. Allow that knowledge to determine how you spend money. Use those principles to help you determine how much money to take out of the business.

The knowledge you gain will also provide a unique perspective regarding customers. I no longer assume the customer in the big house is wealthy. I do not judge customers by appearances. This mentality alone can make your business unique.

Several years ago I went to purchase a car. I had done my homework and saved my money. I was prepared to pay cash for the vehicle. I intentionally wore a T-shirt, blue jeans, and tennis shoes when I went shopping. I expected that only a green salesman would bother working with me (I probably didn't fit their stereotype of a serious buyer).

I spent twenty minutes in the lot at the first dealership and not one salesman spoke to me. I left and went to another dealership. I did buy a car that day. I paid cash. The person who was smart enough not to judge me by my appearance got the deal.

Learn everything you can about money. Find a role model for how you would like to handle money (my brother Josh is mine). Use those principles to make your business successful and reduce your stress. Do not allow yourself to fall into the trap of judging others by their material possessions or wealth. A strong understanding of the importance of making money and investing it wisely builds a strong company.

THOUGHT-PROVOKING QUESTIONS AND ACTION PLANS

1. Did an incident in your early years shape your attitude about money, for better or for worse?

2. What was your parents' attitude and approach to finances? Did they teach you to manage money?

3. On a scale of 1 to 10, are you making the amount of money you want to make? What is helping you or holding you back as it relates to generating income? Have you possibly become content with your income level? Should you be challenging yourself to have higher aspirations?

4. Have you educated yourself about finances? What books have you read about the subject? What courses have you taken? What mentors have you talked to about how they generated wealth?

5. Success is often defined as being rich and famous. Are you more concerned with looking successful to others or with building wealth?

Competition and Comparison

Forget your opponents, always play against par.
—GOLF LEGEND SAM SNEAD

MY FIRST COMPETITION was with my sister, Cyndi. Cyndi was five and I was seven. We would each color a picture in our coloring books, then run to our parents and beg them to judge our work. After a few moments of contemplative silence, they would declare a winner. Imagine that—competitive coloring.

In the beginning competitive coloring was fun. Eventually anxiety built as I realized I was losing some times (knowing my parents it was probably exactly 50 percent of the time). My focus changed from coloring a beautiful picture to beating my little sister. I was miserable when I lost. The game was no longer fun.

Losing in life or business can be depressing too. There have been times when I thrived on beating a specific competitor. It provided a tremendous motivation but often it provided a tremendous angst as well. I found myself concentrating on the competition in lieu of focusing on our operation.

Bernice Berry says, "Curiosity didn't kill the cat, comparison did." We have all had negative feelings toward others and ourselves because we compared their attributes to ours. *I wish I had his muscles. I wish I had her tan. I wish I had her fancy house.*

Exceptional businesses are run by leaders who have a strong desire to be the best. They are not content with mediocre results or mediocre salaries. We need to study the competition in order to create realistic goals. If we aren't conscious of the competition we may be content with mediocre results. We never want to become complacent. I have learned over the years that I am happier when I look at the competition for basic learning. After studying the competition, we turn our focus toward our own objectives—instead of thriving on beating someone.

I have found it is extremely challenging to focus on beating ourselves. Once we determine what critical variables we are going to track, we try to have our best year ever in each category. This is easier said than done. Constantly competing against ourselves challenges us and keeps the atmosphere positive.

Living in an atmosphere of constant competition and comparison can create unhealthy attitudes. I choose to also create a synergistic atmosphere for the employees, using team goals and team recognition. We look at individual production but realize that individual goals create an atmosphere of competition among the employees. I would prefer to have them working together, inspiring each other to achieve the team goals.

Design a business where the team works together to fulfill goals. Be very conscious as to whether or not there are any systems in the business that cause unhealthy competition. Encourage a healthy competition inside the organization and with the outside world.

THOUGHT-PROVOKING QUESTIONS AND ACTION PLANS

1. Are you a competitive person? On a scale of 1 to 10, how important is it to you to be the best at what you do? Explain.

2. Think of a time you competed against others and came out on top. How did that make you feel? What aspect of that success gave you the most satisfaction? How do you think the competition felt?

3. Do you and the people in your office compete against other businesses? Does that impact you in a healthy or an unhealthy way? Explain.

4. How could you and your employees compete against yourselves so the goal is to be your best?

5. Are you overly competitive in other aspects of your life? Do you know people who are cutthroat in sports, with hobbies, or in the financial arena?

Every Day Is Plan B

When the rate of change inside an organization is slower than the rate of change outside the organization, the end is near.
—Jack Welch

IN THE FANTASY world we would be able to create a business plan and have everything fall perfectly into place. Strategic planning can create delusions of invincibility. Reality is quite different. I saw a bumper stick not too long ago that said, "We plan, God laughs." Touché—No matter how well you plan, things will go wrong.

Inherently, we as humans do not typically enjoy the changes that life throws at us. I personally would prefer that I could create a business plan in January and everything would go exactly as I envisioned it throughout the year.

An uncanny focus on the desired destination is key to success. I need to put my business on autopilot by being deliberate in moving toward a preset destination. I must also be able to realign quickly when the business unexpectedly gets thrown off course. An ideal business has a clear vision of its objectives and empowers employees who are prepared to make decisions to consistently move the business toward the goal.

The reality is, every day is Plan B. Top leaders thrive on change instead of becoming disoriented by it. I need to dispel the thought that everything is supposed to go exactly as planned.

I crave change. When things are going smoothly it is more difficult to stand out among the competition. We must constantly look for ways to differentiate our business from others in the industry. Disruptions in our industry make it easier for us to distinguish our business and excel. I stay on my toes by embracing the challenge when things are not going as planned.

Almost every industry is cyclical. There are good times and there are bad times. For many business owners there is the feeling that we are playing a game where we do not get to make the rules. The winners are those who adapt quickly and get back on track.

I actually use challenges to inspire my team. We remember that many businesses stop marketing and stop making cold calls when the going gets tough. That often provides us with a competitive advantage because we continue to market and cold call *while* we're busy. While the competition is crying because things are not going as planned, we are talking to their customers.

A key to thriving during change is constantly honing your skills. Find time to read industry journals, national newspapers, and other related articles. Eric Hoffer said, "In times of change, the learner will inherit the earth while the learned are beautifully equipped for a world that no longer exists." I accept that regardless of the strength of the plan, things will not go as planned.

THOUGHT-PROVOKING QUESTIONS AND ACTION PLANS

1. How do you react when things are not going as planned? Do you respond quickly when business conditions change?

2. How does the team react when changes are required? How do you inspire the team to have a positive perspective on change?

3. Do you function inside of a business or industry where you feel that you do not have full control of the rules of the game? How well does your business adapt when the rules are changed by someone else (e.g., legislation, parent company, etc.)?

4. When you are forced to look at Plan B, do you naturally go back and revisit your business plan? Do you communicate with mentors to determine how they may provide insight to help you through the tough times?

If It Works—Don't Quit

We do not quit playing because we grow old,
we grow old because we quit playing.
—Oliver Wendell Holmes

WHEN YOU GET the business operating ideally, there is always the possibility that the autopilot business will go off-track. We need to be conscious that we are off-track so we can realign quickly.

For many years we operated like a well-oiled machine. Success seemed to come fairly easily. Then some changes in the industry caused major stress. Radical changes in our products were necessary, which forced us to reeducate ourselves and all of our existing clients regarding their coverage. We ceased some of our normal operations for an entire year to make these adjustments.

We were really glad when the twelve months of chaos were over. As the stress reduced, we slowly got back to normal operations. It was many months later that we realized that we had stopped some important processes that had originally brought us tremendous success.

During the time of chaos we had to make adjustments. Unfortunately when the chaos was over we had to realign to get the momentum moving back toward our target. We thought back to our original operation and made a list of the processes that we had stopped doing. We studied these processes to determine whether or not they should be reincorporated into our business.

Having processes defined in writing allowed us to easily reevaluate and realign. We realized that we had actually stopped doing some of the things that brought us success in the first place.

Many things can happen to throw the business off-course temporarily. A tremendous influx of work, changes in market conditions, or the loss of an employee can reduce the effectiveness of a business. Be careful to make sure you do not accidentally eliminate what made you successful initially. Do not quit doing what got you to where you are.

THOUGHT-PROVOKING QUESTIONS AND ACTION PLANS

1. Think back to when your business was new. Are there any processes that caused success then which have now been discontinued?

2. When was the last time your business got thrown off its normal operation? How long did it take you to realign?

3. When you lose an employee does your business realign quickly? Is the bottom line affected radically if you lose one person?

4. Does your business fluctuate radically from month to month? Do you have systems in place to make sure the team regains momentum quickly during down times?

Part 3

TEAM ON TARGET

Plan Ahead, Hire Ahead

There can't be a crisis. My schedule is full.
—HENRY KISSINGER

WHEN I BEGAN my own business, I hired two employees even though we did not have a single customer. I needed only one but thought that twice as many employees would help me reach the goals twice as fast.

Lou Adler, author of *Hire with Your Head*, identifies the two biggest hiring mistakes of most employers:

- Making decisions based on emotional reactions
- Making decisions out of desperation due to waiting until you need someone

I have certainly been guilty of making emotional decisions when hiring. I would ignore red flags or lack of stability in employment history. I have been guilty of falling in love first, then determining whether or not a candidate is qualified.

The second mistake should never happen. As a business owner I need to determine when my business will have grown enough that I may need the next employee. Ideally I will hire that employee before I need him or her.

I envisioned the number of employees my business would eventually have. Once I had that many employees, it never occurred to me that I would have to hire more people. As the number of customers grew, the workload became more demanding. Then the unthinkable happened. Three of my employees were pregnant at the same time. Since we were not adequately staffed, we really felt the pinch when each went on maternity leave.

Originally it seemed perfectly logical to wait until everyone in the office was working at maximum capacity to hire. I learned that waiting until we were overwhelmed was a formula for disaster. Now we have a hiring plan instead of merely winging it. Here are a couple of the criteria:

- Review the business plan and growth goals to determine if you have adequate staffing to meet your goals.
- Build in a cushion for Murphy's Law. It is tempting to put off hiring an additional person until you have a full workload for him or her. Unfortunately, new personnel can increase stress levels and cause productivity to decrease temporarily as you train.

If you wait until you desperately need another employee, you'll put a tremendous amount of stress on everyone involved. Furthermore, Murphy's Law says that one of your current employees will decide to stay home with a new baby, or move, and then you will be even further behind.

Of course you must determine whether or not you can afford another person. Criteria to consider include your fixed and variable expenses as well as the market conditions and your ability to grow the business. If you have been tracking your costs and income, you should be able to determine your break-even number so this can be a pragmatic decision based on facts instead of emotions.

Allow one employee to become fully trained before hiring the next. Attempting to get two people trained simultaneously can be extremely stressful. Your hiring plan should include holding on to existing employees if at all possible (assuming they are productive). I know business owners that lay off employees when the conditions are less than desirable. That is insane behavior if you will have to hire and train another person down the road.

I once saw a bumper sticker that said, "It wasn't raining when Noah built the ark." Exactly. The time to add staff is not when you are overwhelmed by a flood of business or in the middle of a crisis. It is important to me that I can promise customers that we will remain adequately staffed so that we can take care of them immediately when they call.

Plan ahead and hire ahead, and you'll be prepared to handle your clients with quality care that will keep them coming back. Create a strong hiring plan and do not wait until the team is overwhelmed to hire.

THOUGHT-PROVOKING QUESTIONS AND ACTION PLANS

1. Have you ever worked for a business that had a roller-coaster hiring policy—laying off people in the tough times and hiring people in the good times? How did that affect productivity and morale? How did that affect the level of service that the customers received?

2. Have you ever worked for a business that waited until everyone was completely overwhelmed before adding new staff? How did that impact employees? How did that impact clients?

3. Have you ever hired more than one inexperienced person? Did you regret the stress level as you tried to get two employees trained simultaneously?

4. Do you have measurable criteria about when it is time to hire?

5. What is one specific way you will make your hiring process more proactive?

6. Do you promise customers that someone will drop everything immediately and assist them if they call into or come by your office? Are you adequately staffed to fulfill that promise?

The Best One Is Not Looking

Leaders don't force people to follow—
they invite them on a journey.
—Charles S. Lauer

FINDING AND KEEPING quality employees seems to be the most common concern of small-business owners. Most business owners whom I have consulted with are not adequately staffed to achieve their stated goals.

When I speak to these understaffed owners, the number-one excuse I hear is "there aren't any good employees out there." There are quality candidates but unfortunately the best may not be out in the market looking for a new career.

The problem is not that there aren't any good employees but that there aren't any good bosses. Seldom do employers provide a compelling reason for prospective employees to leave their current jobs. In addition, many employers are not comfortable recruiting and interviewing employees. They passively wait for prospective employees to come to them. I can post an ad at my business, in a local newspaper, on a paid Internet site, or on a government site. Then I have to wait and pray that a qualified candidate comes to me.

Just as it is crucial that I hire ahead of my need, it is also crucial that I am constantly looking for the next quality team member. Hiring and retaining quality people is a full-time endeavor. I remain conscious of my responsibility to proactively look for potential candidates. If I am impressed by the strong interpersonal skills of the bank teller I deal with, I make a note of her name. When I am visiting the drugstore at night I am conscious of who goes out of their way to make sure customers are taken care of.

The best candidates are often not in the market for a new job; they may not be unemployed. I need to find them and sell them on the benefits of buying into the dream I am working toward.

I always start by telling them that I can tell they enjoy what they do. I explain that I own a business and I seldom meet someone who provides exceptional customer service. I tell them that I would appreciate the chance to provide them with information on my business opportunity. By proactively searching for exceptional people and being willing to sell the value of my career opportunity, I am increasing my chances of success.

In addition to searching out exceptional people in your day-to-day encounters, you can find success with the following:

- Referrals from employees, friends, and customers. I alert every person I come in contact with that I have a career opportunity. I am very specific about the characteristics we are looking for (I always mention ambitious, stable, and career-minded). My team members would love to handpick the people whom they will be working with.

- Clubs/organizations. Post an ad at the gym, in your church bulletin, or with any other organizations that you are associated with.

- Temporary firms. I have brought in temporary employees to fill a need and found that the person was an ideal candidate for full-time employment.

- Recent college graduates. I am a firm believer that a person who has recently obtained a college degree is often anxious to prove him- or herself in the "real world." They are often very ambitious and disciplined. Most colleges have a service to help place students.

- Job websites. People searching for employment through a website are typically computer literate. That may be preferable depending on the job opening.
- Headhunters. Often a headhunter will have a pool of candidates to choose from. They are professionals at proactively looking for ideal candidates.
- Want ads. This is typically my last resort. I have found some of my best employees through the newspaper but I also had to weed through a tremendous number of bad candidates to find a good one.

Looking for the next right person requires a proactive mindset. Know that the recruiting process is proactive and the best candidates often are not looking. You need to find them.

THOUGHT-PROVOKING QUESTIONS AND ACTION PLANS

1. Is your business currently understaffed? Do you consider it difficult to find good prospective employees?

2. What has been the source of your best employees?

3. Are you proactively looking for potential employees as you move through your day? Do you make a note of exceptional people whom you may want to consider recruiting later?

4. What has been your biggest frustration with the recruiting process? How can you overcome that frustration?

5. Who have you done business with in the last week that could potentially be a good prospect for you? How would you approach him or her with your job opportunity?

The Last Job You Will Ever Have

*I have yet to find a company that has earned high levels of cus-
tomer loyalty without first earning high levels of employee loyalty.*
—FREDERICK REICHHELD

M Y DREAM IS to create an emotionally and financially rewarding environment so no employee will ever want to leave. I tell all prospective
employees, "This is the last job you will ever have. It is my responsibility to
create an opportunity and atmosphere that you would be crazy to leave."

There is a perception among employers and employees that every
employer/employee relationship is temporary. Employers and employees
alike expect the situation will last for a few years at best—then the employee
will become bored or dissatisfied. The perception typically is that this is your
"next" job. This defeatist mentality is unnecessary.

There are several reasons contributing to the mentality that businesses have
a revolving door for employees. Very few employers have tremendous loyalty.
The erosion of trust created by layoffs and downsizing is significant. It is no
wonder that employees feel little loyalty when it is perceived that many employ-

ers are not loyal. Employers have to be reluctant to go into survival mode and cut employees. In addition, employees often feel the grass is greener when they feel they must leave to get additional money, training, or opportunities.

What is the key to drastically improving the satisfaction level for everyone involved? Before the interview begins, design the job. Be very clear about what characteristics are needed for the opening you have. In addition, be very clear about what differentiates your career opportunity from others in the market. Have a stronger understanding of exactly what will be necessary for your potential candidate to be drawn to your job.

The types of job characteristics that would attract the ideal candidate may include:

- Leader with a clear vision of what it takes to succeed
- Strong foundation including a business plan and employee handbook
- System that compensates employees based on their efforts
- Training that empowers employees to be equipped to handle any situation
- Investment in long-term education of employees
- Reasonable job security
- Benefits that are more attractive than those offered by other employers
- Clear line of sight for employees as to how their duties tie to company goals
- Company that has clear expectations and holds people accountable
- Organization that builds trust through communication and consistent feedback
- Leader who accepts responsibility when things are going wrong and acts quickly

Enthusiastic employees are essential. They are the best investment you can make in the healthy growth of a business. The first two people I hired actually took a cut in pay to come work with me. Talk about a sales job! They became extremely enthusiastic as I convinced them that this was a risk that would pay off for them. How did I convince them to do this? Through my own genuine, rock-solid conviction that joining our business was going to be the best career decision they ever made. I could not afford elaborate salaries or bonuses. I had to persuade my team that I would invest in them long term. This persuasion process should be taking place throughout the hiring process.

Understand there is a power shift in the hiring process. When the interview process begins, the employer holds the cards. The employer begins by weeding out unacceptable prospects. Eventually there is a time in which the employer decides a specific prospect is someone who would be a good potential employee. As the prospective employee becomes aware that she is one of the final candidates, there is often a shift in power. The candidate realizes that the employer wants to work with her and final negotiations begin.

If you have done a great job of selling the job prior to this shift, the employee will be excited about the job opportunity. If you have not done a good job then you now have to start selling your job. If you haven't already sold the job a candidate may get cocky as she feels she is now holding the cards.

I have to clearly articulate why a candidate should be drawn to a career opportunity within my organization. I also need to make sure that the uniqueness I am describing is real. Periodically I need to do a gut check. Am I really following through on all of the promises? If I am not sure, I can ask the employees. They will be honest.

Not only do I have to create a career opportunity to encourage employee longevity but I also need to look for red flags of disloyal personalities. Employers look for stability when reviewing resumes of candidates. It is absolutely one of the strongest indicators of employee loyalty. If a potential employee has had three jobs in the last three years without some solid, verifiable explanation, I am not interested. A frequent job change is an indication of a "grass is always greener" mentality.

I also try to verify explanations of job instability. One employee told me that she was unemployed as she cared for a terminally ill parent. I found out later that the gap in employment was really by choice (she was sitting at home on unemployment) and her father had died years earlier.

History can be a strong indication of future. Find candidates who will be loyal and give them a reason to be loyal to you. I must communicate the uniqueness of my job opportunity so ideal candidates are attracted.

THOUGHT-PROVOKING QUESTIONS AND ACTION PLANS

1. Do you have a job that offers unique opportunities? Do you communicate your uniqueness to potential employees?

2. Do you specifically design the job prior to beginning interviews? Are expectations clear in your mind prior to interviews and articulated succinctly during the process?

3. Have you ever felt the power shift in the interview process? Have you done a good enough job of communicating the value of the opportunity prior to the candidate's realizing you are ready to make a job offer?

4. Does your organization have a culture of synergy or scarcity? Do team members work together to achieve company goals?

5. Does your business have an ongoing value proposition for employees? Are there reasons to hang on long term? Do you continue to sell the benefits of working in your organization after the employees have been with you for an extended period?

Who Are You, Really?

*When I interview people, and they give me an immediate
answer, they're often not thinking. So I'm silent. I wait.*
—Robin Leach

In his book *Good to Great* Jim Collins communicates that before you
determine a specific strategy for the business you need to make sure you
have the right people on the bus. Easier said than done! It takes time to find
the right employees. Many employers get on-the-job training on how to
select teammates. Unfortunately, I learned the hard way not to hire people
solely because they interviewed well. Anyone can pretend to care for the
length of time it takes to interview for a job. But having a strong interview
process increases the chances that the type of person you think you are getting is actually what you get.

I have now learned not to make emotional decisions. I systematically go
through the same basic process each time I have a job opening. The process
goes as follows:

- **Design the job.** Originally I would hire someone, wait a few months to see what he/she was good at, and then realign responsibilities based on the employee's strengths. My job would then be to do all of the tasks my employee was not good at. My job was created by default and I was not always doing what I was good at. Now we design the job, determine what strengths are necessary, and do not hire until we find someone that fits the bill. A clear job description with specific expectations needs to exist prior to any interviews.

- **Take applications and resumes.** We require that all applicants come into the office to complete an application. You can find standardized employment applications at office supply stores. Every applicant completes the same exact application and some will provide a resume, which may provide additional information. Resumes with major typographical errors or sloppy format can indicate lazy behavior.

- **Evaluate personality scores.** Several years ago I found a book that provided tremendous insight into how a person's personality type can be an indicator of behavior at work. Marita and Florence Littauer's *Wired That Way* discusses basic personality types. Understanding personality types allows me to know something about a person prior to interviewing them. This reduces the chances that I will hire emotionally.

  I have candidates take the personality test when they complete the employment application. By providing this exam to potential applicants I can easily see some potential strengths and weaknesses, which takes some of the guesswork out of hiring. Test results also allow me to anticipate areas that could cause concern. I then have the ability to address them prior to hiring or to keep looking for the right candidate.

- **Provide applicant with a copy of our employee handbook.** I want every person being considered for employment to understand what we are about. The employee handbook communicates our mission, job descriptions, compensation information, and basic office organization. The potential employee is provided a copy of the employee handbook at the time they complete the employee application. I tell every applicant to call once they have read the employee handbook; we will then schedule an interview. When the potential employee takes more than a couple of days to get back to us, it indicates to me they may not be anxious to get the job. Some candidates will not call for the interview once they have read the handbook and understand the job they are applying for. If it is not right for them, I would prefer that they deselect early.

- **Listen for a good phone voice.** You have probably heard the saying "You never get a second chance to make a first impression." In many businesses the first contact with a potential customer is made over the phone. If a prospective employee has a nasal, shrill, or screechy voice, she could alienate a customer. If she has a soft, little girl voice, she may not inspire the necessary confidence. If he is difficult to hear, has a monotone voice, or uses too much slang, he will not make a favorable phone impression. A pleasing and professional-sounding voice is priceless. When the potential employee calls to schedule the first interview, I am listening for the quality of her voice.

- **Give points for professional appearance.** Pay close attention to what type of attire each candidate wears to the interviews. I have actually had people show up for a job interview in shorts or jeans with holes in them. If a prospect does not care enough to dress to impress for an interview, he is certainly not going to care enough to dress appropriately for his day-to-day job.

- **Require realistic compensation expectations.** I have turned down several quality applicants over the years because their salary expectations were not realistic. This typically happens if someone has relocated from a city that has a much higher cost of living or if the applicant is changing industries. I have never met anyone who was happy taking a cut in pay, even if their living expenses were reduced. I personally had to deal with taking a cut in pay years ago when I moved to an area that had lower salaries and a lower cost of living. I never got over the resentment. I ask prospective employees about salary expectations and what the salary was at their most recent job. This allows me to determine whether or not the position I have open is in a reasonable salary range for this candidate.

- **Check references.** I do not contact personal references. Surely anyone can find three or four people to say something nice about them. I do call prior employers. A former employer has limitations as to what information can be shared. I have had prior employers share inappropriate information such as "He does drugs" or "Her mom had her thrown in jail for stealing." You can often get valuable information from a former employer by things they *do not* say. Often the tone of the prior employer's voice will provide hints as to the type of experience they had with this person. Common sense will typically provide red flags if there is an issue. Use due diligence in researching work history to be confident that the credentials on the resume are real and not exaggerated.

- **Look for positive answers to open-ended questions.** It amazes me that some employers make snap decisions and bring someone into their organization following a fifteen-minute interview. A successful job interview should take more than fifteen minutes and allow the prospective employee to do most of the talking. Often interviewers dominate the conversation and try to sell the applicant on the open position. Ask open-ended questions such as "What did you like or dislike about your previous job?" People will often reveal their true personality when answering these wide-open questions. If they focus only on how unappreciated and overworked they were and what a jerk their boss was, it tells you a lot about their personality. If they have only negative things to say, it will only be a matter of time before they are complaining about you.

- **Invite fellow employees to chime in.** Prior to making my decision, I have the candidate meet with a current employee. There are two primary reasons for this. First, I want the team to feel comfortable with the new hire. In addition, I want the new employee to have the ability to feel comfortable he is making the right decision. I have found that the candidate will ask questions of my employees that he is afraid to ask me. In the back of his mind there may be a fear it could jeopardize his chances of obtaining the job. Before a decision is made I ask one of my less-tenured employees to visit with the potential employee. I make sure everyone feels comfortable that no subject is off limits. The meeting between those two parties is a closed-door meeting and I never pump my employee for information afterward.

I genuinely want the candidate to be provided a realistic perspective prior to making a decision.

- **Require detailed personality analysis.** Everyone I hire, including part-time employees, undergoes a detailed personality analysis. At this stage I need a test that is more detailed, oriented toward characteristics that are specific to the job opening. Personality tests allow matching ideal candidates and understanding personality strengths and weaknesses.

- **Conduct final interview.** I typically will have one last interview after receiving the detailed personality analysis. This is a good time to bring up any potential concerns that may have been uncovered by the testing. Personality tests are used to match jobs, not used as ammunition to fix people. This is the last opportunity to make sure that expectations are clear and the candidate and position are a match.

Once I have the right person on board it helps when I follow these steps:

1. Continue to reinforce expectations. Get employees up and running as soon as possible. Be very specific about expectations.

2. Assign a mentor in the office. I personally prefer to do as much training as possible, but it is important to assign a specific employee to play "mother hen" to support new hires so they feel welcome and informed.

3. Use a training schedule so new hires are brought up to speed in all activities in a timely way. Previously we trained new hires as each process came up in the day-to-day job. Sometimes employees worked for us for a year before they learned how to deal with certain less-used products. A proactive training program provides a well-rounded education.

4. Check in frequently with new hires. This gives the new hire an opportunity to communicate if there are challenges.

Hiring and on-boarding an employee requires an investment. It is important to take the time to find the person who will make a valuable addition to your team. Make the process extensive enough so that you get a realistic perspective on the candidate's potential. I am willing to spend the time to increase the odds that the person I think I know is actually the person who shows up for work.

THOUGHT-PROVOKING QUESTIONS AND ACTION PLANS

1. Do you have a system for conducting interviews that determine how a person would fit into your team? Describe it.

2. How important is a good voice in your industry? How do you determine if a prospective employee will project a pleasant, professional-sounding voice to clients?

3. Are you conscious of the appearance of prospective employees when they come for an interview?

4. Do you have a policy about checking references? What is that? Was there a time you did not check references and regretted it? What happened?

5. Are you willing to make the financial investment necessary to do a good personality analysis? If you don't spend that money, what might a bad hire cost you?

If You Are Not Like Me—
I Like You

Never hire or promote in your own image. It is foolish to replicate your strength and idiotic to replicate your weakness. It is essential to employ, trust, and reward those whose perspective, ability, and judgment are radically different from yours. It is also rare, for it requires uncommon humility, tolerance, and wisdom.
—Dee W. Hock

My ORIGINAL HIRING formula was not sophisticated. I would look for happy people whom I thought I would enjoy spending the day with. Later we would figure out what they were capable of. You may be thinking, "You have got to be kidding." I wish I were.

My first employee was a petite young woman whose previous job was walking door to door selling copy machines. She stopped in to sell me a copy machine and I sold her on a new career instead. There was no formal interview. I was blessed to find a tremendous employee in spite of the fact that I had no idea how to hire.

Several months later I was at a party and a young woman and I exchanged pleasantries. I asked her what type of work she did and she informed me that she was working as a manager of a drugstore. She was responsible for the night shift. You guessed it! She became my second employee.

Instead of looking for people whom I had a lot in common with, I should have been looking for people who complemented me. I had no idea how important it was to put together a diverse team. I trained the employees myself and became familiar with their strengths and weaknesses (this was before I used personality-testing systems). I assigned them responsibility based on my unscientific observations. Guess who got to do the tasks no one was good at? *Me!*

I was specifically looking for people like me. I thought if I hired people who were like me, we would enjoy working together.

Peter Drucker said, "It is not your job to like employees or to change employees. Your job is to determine their strengths and put them to work." It is important that the team is made up of people who can work together well. The team does not, however, have to consist of people whom you would choose to socialize with on the weekends. This is business and any business is stronger if it is diverse.

Both employees did exceptionally well in spite of my haphazard hiring process. I was lucky. If I had it to do over again, my hiring process would not hinge on whether a potential employee's personality was similar to mine. I need to attract candidates who have strengths to offset the current team's weaknesses.

Many business owners are great at sales but still need to hire great managers. Many business owners are great managers and organizers but do not necessarily enjoy sales. Design your job so that you are able to work within your strengths and hire others to do the tasks that you are not good at. I choose to embrace a team that is diverse so the team has varying talents.

THOUGHT-PROVOKING QUESTIONS AND ACTION PLANS

1. Look at the makeup of the people you work with today. Do you tend to look for employees who are like you or employees who complement you?

2. What is the biggest weakness in your current team? When will you be in a position to search for someone who has the characteristics needed to offset that weakness?

3. Do you find you prefer to spend time with people who have personalities that are similar to yours? When you are exposed to someone who frustrates you, contemplate whether or not you should be more tolerant of your personality differences.

4. Do you encourage and respect differing opinions? Are your employees convinced that you respect their opinions even when they differ from yours? Does your organization encourage communication and creativity?

5. Do you consider yourself better as a manager or as a salesperson? Do you have others within the organization who are strong in the area where you are weaker?

Put People's Personalities to the Test

Ninety percent of the world's woes come from peo-
ple not knowing themselves, their abilities, their frail-
ties, and even their real virtues. Most of us go almost all
the way through life as complete strangers to ourselves.
—SYNDEY J. HARRIS

TO PARAPHRASE SYDNEY Harris, I think 90 percent of a company's woes come from not knowing the abilities, frailties, and virtues of its personnel, including those of owners and managers. When I ask employers what their biggest challenge is, the answer is typically personnel issues. Within a properly structured business, employees are not the source of problems; they are the solution to them.

Personality testing allows me to do a better job of hiring the right person. The tests are also extremely beneficial when I have to assign responsibilities initially or after a transition.

I started by testing myself. I needed to design my job first, knowing what I was best at. With the help of professionals I could see which tasks I was best suited for. I became a student of personality testing. Originally I did not enjoy studying personalities. Eventually I understood why. When I studied personality testing, my focus was on my weaknesses. I really didn't want to think about my weaknesses.

Marcus Buckingham and Donald O. Clifton's book *Now, Discover Your Strengths* was a turning point for me. This book provides a unique perspective that we should spend time enhancing people's strengths rather than eliminating weaknesses—novel idea!

I eventually realized that I was much better off spending my time focusing on my strengths instead of my weaknesses. I could design a job where my job duties matched my personality strengths. No one is good at everything. I don't have to be superwoman. I could focus on what I am good at and hire others to do the rest.

I find many business owners are reluctant to do personality testing. They fear that they will have to deal with their weaknesses or be told they are not appropriate for self-employment. Let me give you a hint—you are the right person for the job. Don't worry about what you are not good at. You can find someone to do what you are not good at.

We have a tendency to compare our weaknesses to other people's strengths. I cannot allow myself to become overly involved in comparing myself to others. I use personality testing as a pragmatic way to design my job and attract applicants with the right strengths for the position I have open.

Our strength taken to an extreme becomes our weakness. In other words, being kind is a wonderful quality. However, being so kind that we let people walk all over us is surely detrimental. If we are assertive and comfortable asking for what we want, that is a healthy thing. But if we are so aggressive we end up caring *only* about what we want, that is not healthy. A thorough person is wonderful; an overly thorough person can become such a perfectionist that nothing ever gets finished.

I tested every full-time and part-time person once I realized how much more effectively we operated with this additional information. After identifying our relative strengths and weaknesses, we reassigned some responsibilities. Within weeks, we experienced a boost in productivity because we were all doing the work we were best at.

I also made sure to assign the leftover jobs that had formerly been bequeathed to me because no one else was good at them. There were still a few tasks that did not fit any of our strengths. Guess what we did with those? We kept a list of the weaknesses left in the office. The next time we had an opportunity to hire a new person, we did not hire until we found a person who would be a good fit for those jobs.

If you are concerned about the costs involved with personality testing, just ask yourself, "How much does it cost to advertise, interview, hire, and train a new staff member? How much does it cost to lose the person months later because she was not suited for the position? Then you have to start the hiring process all over again."

Once you calculate the costs in terms of time, money, training, and frustration, the expense of personality testing is a wonderful investment. Study the unique personality strengths and weaknesses of each candidate to build a strong team.

THOUGHT-PROVOKING QUESTIONS AND ACTION PLANS

1. Have you ever taken a personality test? What did you learn about yourself, and how did you apply that knowledge in the workplace?

2. Does your business use personality testing in the hiring process? If so, how has this impacted your ability to find the right applicant for the job?

3. Are your current employees given personality tests to determine their strengths and weaknesses? How has this impacted the assignment of tasks? Has this made a difference in the office productivity and morale?

4. If you do not have personality testing, how are you going to research this to determine if it is a viable option for your business? Notice I did not mention disposing of employees not ideally suited. This process is to realign duties, not dispose of people.

5. Do you have any strength that you may carry to an unhealthy extreme? Ask your friends or co-workers to confirm your analysis.

Experience Is Not Necessarily a Good Thing

Men are wise in proportion, not to their experience, but to their capacity for experience.
—James Boswell

L IFE IS FULL of experiences that provide insight into business. A trip to London provided one of those opportunities. I was standing in front of Buckingham Palace watching the Queen's Guard. As a horse aficionado, I was particularly interested in the well-trained horses and riders. Imagine my surprise when the tour guide explained that the government preferred to hire people without riding experience to be in the Queen's Guard.

He said, "We have found that experienced riders have bad habits that are hard to break. A person with no riding experience starts from scratch and we can teach them to ride the right way—our way. When we do not have to work around their ingrained way of doing things, the horse and rider become one much faster."

Hmmm. His observation was consistent with my beliefs about the draw-back of hiring staff members with industry experience. Unlike many business owners, I personally prefer to hire people with little or no experience. I am much more concerned with potential than with industry-specific knowledge.

There are advantages and disadvantages to hiring a person who is already experienced in your industry.

Advantages:

- Reduced need for training
- Provide true assistance to the team in less time
- May provide new insight based on their experience

Disadvantages:

- May be job-hopping
- Typically more expensive to hire
- Have more turnover than with staff I trained from scratch
- Walk in with preconceived notions about "the best way" to run things

On more than one occasion, an employee has told me, "That is not the way we did it at my last job." In fact, one new hire told me, "You do it how-ever you want. I am going to do it my way."

I had to tell her, "There is no such thing as 'your way.' We as a team decide the best way to execute each process. Everyone in our office follows that process identically." Taking time to define the "best way" to complete each process provides a more exceptional and consistent experience for the customer. We welcome suggestions for improvements but cannot have each person determining which procedures they will and will not follow.

If I was opening a business in which I had no industry experience, I would make an exception to the rule. It makes sense to take advantage of someone's experience if you have none. It may also be logical to look for industry experience if you are opening multiple locations. Be careful to remain determined to provide a consistent experience.

Any candidate with the appropriate strengths and a positive attitude can be trained to do the job. Don't be intimidated by the extra time it takes to train an inexperienced person. You will typically have a tremendous payoff tied to lower employee turnover when you are willing to train from scratch. Just remember, the easy way out may not be the smart way out. The best candidate for the job may have no industry experience.

THOUGHT-PROVOKING QUESTIONS AND ACTION PLANS

1. What type and level of experience do you prefer when you are hiring new employees?

2. Have you ever hired an employee who had bad habits? Were you able to make that situation work?

3. Do you have an ongoing educational program? Are employees trained on all aspects of the business?

4. Are you willing to make the investment necessary to train a new employee from scratch? Is there someone in your operation who would be better equipped than you to do the training?

Don't Worry About What
Will Happen if They Leave

If you think education is expensive, try ignorance.
—Message on billboard

EDUCATION IS ONE of the easiest ways to distinguish your business. Being known as a resource in your field radically increases your value. You will also find that your best employees will thrive on being challenged to become more educated. Unfortunately, some business owners are reluctant to support educational opportunities for their employees.

This point was driven home at a presentation I did in Houston, Texas. I was discussing how employee education could improve customer loyalty. During the program a business owner interrupted by asking, "What if I spend a bunch of money educating them and they leave?" I shared something I remembered reading: "Don't worry about what will happen if you train an employee and they leave. Worry about what will happen if you don't train them and they stay."

I would prefer spending time educating than spending time apologizing for sloppy service. It takes a lot of time and money to correct mistakes committed due to lack of knowledge.

I have found that employers typically refuse to educate for one of two reasons—fear or greed. At the age of twenty-five I quit a job because my employer provided absolutely no educational opportunities. In over three years on the job, it became clear that education was not a priority. I could only assume that education was not provided because we would perceive ourselves to be more valuable and they would take a chance on losing us or be forced to increase our pay.

There are employees who will be perfectly content with no opportunities for personal growth—unfortunately they are probably the employees you would be better off without. Strong employees value education and want to work in a learning organization. Your best employees may leave you if they do not perceive education is valued.

I have three designations that are acknowledged by the insurance/financial services industry. I knew the designations would provide me with additional knowledge and credibility in my industry. I did not get the designations to sell more insurance but they have increased the number of referrals that the business receives.

I have had customers say, "I don't know what all of those letters mean but they must mean you are smart." They realize the additional education indicates that we are serious about what we do. Professionals appreciate working with other professionals. Quality clients are more likely to pick your name out of the Yellow Pages or Internet if they see professional designations.

If I have invested in the education of my employees it radically reduces my stress level because it increases their independence. I have no freedom to relax when I leave the office unless I am leaving it in capable hands.

How much money should be spent on each employee? Originally I spent the same amount of money on each employee's education. Over time, I realized it made more sense to spend 2–3 percent of each person's salary each year. My salaries are based on the contribution each person makes to the company. It is just good business to put a commensurate amount of dollars into the education of those employees who are earning more for the business.

Look for free or inexpensive educational opportunities in your community through local colleges or business seminars. Use an education calendar to make sure learning and growing remains a priority long term. Start with basic skills (training on listening, handling tough customers, etc.) and consistently provide product training year after year.

Look for more challenging education for more experienced employees. Challenge them personally and professionally. Provide training that benefits the employees as well as the business (e.g., classes on personal financial management, leadership training, etc.).

Earl Nightingale said, "One extra hour of study per day and you will be a national expert in five years or less." You may not desire to be a national expert but a small amount of effort can make you exceptionally knowledgeable in your field. Investing in the education of employees and leaders builds a strong organization.

THOUGHT-PROVOKING QUESTIONS AND ACTION PLANS

1. If you are a business owner, do you have a policy concerning the education of your employees? What is that? How much do you invest annually in each employee's professional development?

2. Have you wrestled with that "Why pay to train them if they're going to leave" issue? How have you resolved it?

3. When and how are you going to start an education program for yourself and your staff?

4. Are you a member of professional associations in your industry? Are you utilizing the continuing education from the associations to further your education? Are you growing from associating with other professionals in your industry? Do they send you referrals?

5. How will you budget funds for the education of employees? Will they all receive the same education?

Education Goes Only so Far

To know and not to do—is not to know at all.
—Goethe

I ADMIT IT—I AM an information junkie. I love learning. After singing the praises of education, it is important to add a caveat. Education is important, but it is not enough. If we do not act on what we have learned, education is for naught.

Early in my career, I was addicted to learning. I have my mom to thank for that. She inspired me to crave intelligence. She was a walking encyclopedia. People would say, "Claudine knows everything!" I admired the fact that she was respected for her knowledge.

In my twenties I was lucky enough to work for a wonderful man who told me I would never amount to anything. Really! He basically told me I was going to be a loser.

After the shock of his statement sunk in, he proceeded with, "You will never amount to anything because you never finish anything. You started martial arts and never got your black belt. You started college and never finished." I loved learning and I was a great idea person but I wasn't always as enthusiastic with execution. Mr. McClure was right. I would never amount to anything unless I learned to finish what I started.

I spent the next few years finishing everything he mentioned that had been left incomplete. Yes, I got my black belt, finished college, and much more.

I still love to learn but now I am careful to implement the things I have learned. In those first few years of running my business, I read at least one business book a week. I would identify what I thought was our biggest weakness. If that happened to be marketing, I would read several marketing books until I felt comfortable with my level of knowledge on the subject.

Although I still crave education, and I still seek out good books, I have learned to value execution equally. Burying myself in a book and being a perpetual student can be a cop out. I know that knowledge without action is irrelevant. Great ideas unexecuted have little value. As Henry Ford said, "You can't build a reputation on what you are going to do." Eventually you have to get up and go.

My insatiable need to learn became a focused determination to turn the knowledge into action. My future is determined by the decisions I am making today and the actions I am or am not taking today. As soon as I finish a section in a book, I put it down and ask myself, "What is one thing I am going to start, stop, or do differently as a result of reading this?"

I contemplate the implications of the learning on my varying roles. What does that book teach me that will make me a better parent? A better employer? A better church or association member? I want to gain information from books and other resources. Eventually, however, I have to get out of the self-help section of the library and get to work on applying what I have learned.

The next time you read a book or attend a seminar, commit to applying at least one principle that you've learned. Sharpening the saw is great but eventually you have to use it. Education without action is of little value.

THOUGHT-PROVOKING QUESTIONS AND ACTION PLANS

1. Do you like to read business or self-help books? Do you have a favorite that has had a long-lasting impact on you? Why did it have such an effect on you?

2. Are you lopsided in your learning? If you find yourself reading only for pleasure, pick up a business book. If you find yourself reading only business books, pick up a novel you can relax with. When you become lopsided, force yourself to alternate business reading with pleasure reading.

3. What training program, industry convention, or professional development seminar helped you gain valuable knowledge? How were you able to use what you learned on the job?

4. Does your business have a way to hold employees accountable for putting into practice what they learn from educational programs? What is it?

Never Be Held Hostage

You're only as good as the people you hire.
—Ray Kroc

R AY KROC WAS smart enough to understand that you cannot build a great business without great people. I would take it one step further and say we are only as good as the people we hire *and retain.* I must hire the right people and empower them without abdicating responsibility. I need to train and delegate without losing sight of the day-to-day activities myself.

The quality of our employees determines our success. Great employees accelerate success. Business owners need to ensure that we create a business system where the loss of an employee will not undermine or threaten the stability of the organization.

In 1996, I visited an extremely successful businessman. He bragged about the fact that his employees ran a large portion of his business. He seemed to take pride in his lack of knowledge of that portion of the business. I was immediately concerned about whether or not he might be too dependent upon them. I asked, "Aren't you afraid of what will happen if they leave you?"

"Absolutely not" was his answer. "My employees have been with me for ages. Even if I lost one it would not be a big deal."

Six months later he informed me, "My employees walked out on me. All of them, at once! I feel like I am starting from scratch," he confessed. This business owner had to go back and relearn the basics. It had to have been a humbling experience. I wondered if they left simultaneously to spite him, since they knew it would be painful.

There should never be any process in a business that only one person is trained to perform. Each and every process should be defined in writing and at least two people should be familiar with the operation of that process. There should be no process in the office that the business owner is not familiar with. Also, there should never be a process in the office that only the business owner is familiar with.

Following that eye-opening conversation with my friend who had been left in the lurch, I stopped to consider whether or not I was vulnerable. Unfortunately, I was. That afternoon I informed everyone in my business that we would be undergoing some "basic training." When employees know you are completely dependent upon them, they can "hold you hostage." It is not a good situation for the employee or employer.

It is my responsibility to make sure that employees understand that every person in the organization is invaluable, but there is no person who cannot be replaced. In order for our business to work, everyone must understand we are a team and each individual is only part of the team.

To create a system where no one person feels he or she is superior requires the following steps:

- Initiate a cross-training program where employees teach one another various aspects of the business.

- Provide product training on an annual basis for all basic products. Do not assume that a person you trained ten years ago is completely familiar with the nuances of your products.

- Design a compensation system that rewards employees for exceptional team results. Everyone is working toward a common goal instead of trying to compete with each other, encouraging a harmonious rather than an adversarial office atmosphere.

• Define each process in writing. This eliminates the possibility of an employee holding you hostage because she is the only person who is capable of performing a task. By having all procedures clearly outlined, another employee can take over if needed.

• Promote a culture whereby each employee is required to treat the others with respect. To enforce this principle, I have terminated an employee for repeatedly treating other employees or customers disrespectfully. Employees make a choice to treat each other well or poorly. They can choose to treat each other with respect.

I have a responsibility to design operational systems that reduce stress and ensure more predictable results. Designing systems also increases the consistency with which the services are delivered.

Our team must not be overly dependent on me—nor held hostage by any employee. I must create a business where no one, including myself, is irreplaceable. Employees should not want to be irreplaceable. If they can't be replaced, they can't be promoted. Create viability for the organization by cross-training and not creating irreplaceable people.

THOUGHT-PROVOKING QUESTIONS AND ACTION PLANS

1. Have you ever worked for a business where an employee tested the boundaries and began acting like a prima donna? How did that affect the morale and effectiveness of the rest of the team?

2. Do your employees know more about what goes on in the business than you do? How are you going to retrain yourself and others in operating procedures so you do not have a potentially dangerous situation where an employee can hold everyone hostage?

3. Make a list of each process that requires a person to run it. Ask yourself, "Is a step-by-step explanation outlining exactly how to do that in our operational manual?" If not, how and when are you going to add it to your manual?

4. Look around the office. Identify five different systems—whether it is how to lock up at night, program the phones, do a new business application, or replace the printer cartridge in the copier. Are there any operations that only one person knows how to perform? If so, what will happen if you lose that person?

5. Do you have at least two people who know how to operate all systems? If not, when are you going to schedule a cross-training to bring employees up to speed on how to handle those tasks?

Leave the Problems at the Door

Intellectuals solve problems; geniuses prevent them.
—Albert Einstein

SOME PEOPLE SEEM to thrive on drama. Have you ever worked with someone who appears to worry incessantly that something might go wrong? It is emotionally draining to work with someone who overemphasizes negative issues or seems to create unnecessary stress.

At one time I worked with a woman who would run into my office several times a day and say, "We've got a problem!" It took me months to realize the impact this statement had on me. As soon as she said the words I would become anxious. More often than not, it was not a problem but a question. Nothing was really wrong.

We actually created a rule in our office that the word *problem* is not to be used. It is amazing how eliminating that word reduces stress. For most people, that word means something is wrong. If we use it often enough, it begins to seem that nothing ever goes right.

Now that no one is allowed to use *problem*, we have become sensitized to the damage that little seven-letter word can cause. We have realized people use it habitually. I have been in many meetings where the person in charge wraps things up by asking, "Any other problems we need to discuss before we adjourn?" Why not say, "Is there anything additional we need to discuss before we adjourn?"

You may be thinking, "But what are we supposed to say if we really do have a problem?"

A friend once told me that words are the verbal crayons that color our perceptions. I think the word *problem* can have a tendency to cause panic. The word alone paints a picture that we are facing an insurmountable challenge.

Instead of saying, "I have a problem," try the statement "I have a question." Instead of saying, "I understand you have a problem with your bill," say, "I understand you have some questions about your bill."

I had to stop reinforcing the person who was creating stress. Once she was no longer allowed to use the word *problem,* our stress levels reduced noticeably.

The second part of our program to become problem free required that I stop rescuing my staff. If they came to me with a problem, I would ask them what they felt the best possible solution was.

If necessary I would pose several possible options for handling the situation. I would ask Socratic questions: "Do you think this could work?" or "What is another way to turn this around?" The questions would facilitate their thinking through the situation instead of counting on me to solve it. Almost always, they were able to come up with a viable answer themselves. I also reinforced my faith in their abilities by holding them accountable for going back to the client and handling the situation. I did not swoop in and save them.

Over time, the employees grew more and more comfortable handling issues. Not only did they feel empowered and grow professionally but my workload was also drastically reduced. I had more control of my time because I was not running around putting out fires.

Author and professional speaker Larry Winget says, "Teach your people not to start fires. Teach them to put out their own fires. If this does not work get new people." I have found that by teaching my people how to put out their own fires, I do not need to get new people. Resolve today to become problem free. Vow to stop allowing daily issues to cause drama and negatively impact emotions.

THOUGHT-PROVOKING QUESTIONS AND ACTION PLANS

1. Do you use the word *problem* often? Describe a situation in which you recently used it. How did it make you feel? How did it impact the person you were dealing with?

2. Try to catch yourself in the act of saying the word *problem*. When you do, replace it with a word or phrase that does not mean something is wrong. Notice what a difference it makes in your communication and in your perspective on the world.

3. At your next staff meeting, hold a discussion on how often you use the word *problem*. Discuss the negative perception it may be giving customers.

4. How are you going to create a policy that outlaws the use of the word *problem* in your office? How are you going to hold each other accountable for using words that do not create anxiety?

5. What is your plan to wean staff members from dumping their problems into your lap? How are you going to teach them to think through and resolve challenges themselves?

6. Do you have someone who currently seems to prefer to be in a constant state of crisis? What is the best way to handle this situation?

He Loves Me, He Loves Me Not

*The deepest desire in human nature
is the craving to be appreciated.*
—WILLIAM JAMES

I CONSULTED WITH A business where the owner described serious morale issues in his operation. He said, "I pay more than the industry average, and I give them the latest computers and gadgets. I do not understand why they are so unhappy." For a few hours I watched him in action. He was one of those hyper-critical, "never notice what they do right, always notice what they do wrong" bosses. He was very quick to point out how they could do things faster or more efficiently. He thought he was teaching them, but he was actually demoralizing them because he nitpicked and critiqued every action.

I became exhausted and frustrated just watching him push his employees. I was also able to have one-on-one conversations with the employees. Each complained, "We don't trust him because he doesn't care about us."

When either party loses trust, the relationship is in jeopardy. Unfortunately the boss may have felt a need to control the situation by micromanaging employees because he sensed their lack of trust. The boss was actually a nice guy. Unfortunately his leadership style didn't allow his employees to see that. We talked extensively about the trust issues and his tendency to micromanage employees. I suggested, "Tomorrow, spend the day letting your staff know how much you appreciate all of the things they do well."

He said defensively, "Why should I have to make a big deal about them doing their job? That is what I pay them for. Besides," he said, "I am not comfortable giving compliments. It is just not my style."

I countered with "If you care about them, you will get out of your comfort zone and spend more time emphasizing the positive than the negative." There is an art to giving a good compliment.

- **Make it specific.** Generic statements like "Good job" are perceived as perfunctory and are not taken seriously. It is far more meaningful to make a detailed observation such as "That client was really upset when she walked in. You handled the situation so well that she walked out ten minutes later with a smile on her face. That took skill."

- **Make it immediate.** Saving a list of the good things that employees do for a performance appraisal is crazy. By then, their attitude could have soured because they think no one noticed or cared about their extra efforts. As Ralph Waldo Emerson said, "You cannot do a kindness too soon because you never know how soon it will be too late."

- **Decide when to compliment.** Evaluate whether it is better to give the praise in public or in private. Dr. Haim Ginot said, "If you want children to improve, let them overhear the nice things you say about them to others." Some employees blossom when complimented in front of their peers, some are embarrassed. It might not be appropriate to praise an employee in front of co-workers if he or she will perceive you are playing favorites by singling that person out. On the other hand, it can be beneficial to the team to give kudos publicly if a staff member has achieved something extraordinary and deserves to be applauded for an above-and-beyond performance.

- **Address their suspicion.** If a rather brusque boss started handing out compliments as if they were candy, his team would probably have wondered if he was on his deathbed. He needed to anticipate that his abrupt change in behavior might make them think he had an ulterior motive. It would not hurt to apologize if the ratio of compliments to complaints has been inappropriate.

Most of us get wrapped up in all our obligations and overlook this little nicety. Giving credit where credit is due is not something to be done only in the good times when we are not overwhelmed. It is to be done every day so our employees know their contributions are appreciated.

The good news is when we take the time to give employees the praise they want, need, and deserve, it makes both of us feel good. As Samuel Goldwyn said, "When someone does something good, applaud! You will make two people happy." Provide employees with positive feedback to allow them to feel valued and stay on track.

THOUGHT-PROVOKING QUESTIONS AND ACTION PLANS

1. When was the last time someone went out of his or her way to give you an encouraging word? Do you feel your efforts often go unnoticed and unappreciated? How does that impact you?

2. Are you comfortable giving compliments? Is it in your style to give recognition? Explain.

3. Think of a specific situation in which you recently gave an employee a compliment. What did you say? How did that person respond?

4. Is someone overdue for some recognition or appreciation? How and when are you going to approach that person to give them that overdue compliment?

5. Do you have employees who are uncomfortable being complimented in front of others? How will you make sure that they feel appreciated?

Know the Right Thing to Say

*The real art of conversation is not only to say the
right thing in the right place, but to leave unsaid
the wrong thing at the tempting moment.*
—Dorothy Nevill

A BUSINESS OWNER I worked for years ago once told a client, "I cannot find your file. My secretary probably lost it." Yikes! First of all, it is no longer politically correct to call people *secretaries.* In fact, what used to be the national organization for secretaries, PSI (Professional Secretaries International), changed its name because members felt that term did not indicate or reflect the full scope of their work. It is now called Association for Office Professionals. Referring to someone as a secretary can have a negative connotation for some. Describing my employees as licensed advisors gives them a respected title that makes it clear to clients that they are not simply there to take messages for me. Each person is fully trained and capable of handling any situation.

You can probably guess the other reason that the behavior described above bothered me. It is never acceptable to blame an employee for something you have done. This person *always* had stacks of UPOs (unidentified piled objects) on his desk. My desk, on the other hand, was neat. He preferred making me look bad to admitting he was at fault.

Not only would I have been happier had he admitted fault but I feel the customer would have had more respect for him. No one is comfortable when someone is pointing the blame elsewhere.

Does your trust and respect for an organization plummet when the person you are speaking to does not take responsibility? Imagine a client calls in upset and says, "You were supposed to contact me yesterday to tell me when I would be getting my check." Your first urge might be to come up with an excuse. Don't pass the buck. Understand that the client does not care why you did not get back to him or who is to blame. He wants acknowledgment that you did not carry through as promised and he wants an answer to his original question.

Instead of saying the first thing that comes to mind, take the AAA Train, a technique that Sam Horn describes in her book *Tongue Fu!* It works like this.

- A = Agree. "You are right. I was supposed to call you back yesterday with that information."
- A = Apologize. "And I am sorry I did not get back to you as promised."
- A = Act. "May I put you on hold for a few moments while I find out the status of your check?"

Do you see how the client will now feel you're resolving the situation instead of making excuses?

The next time a customer calls to complain, stop to think about whether or not the complaint is logical. If his complaint is legitimate, do not explain the rules or pass off responsibility. Simply say those magic words, "You are right," and show empathy. Even if you are unable to resolve the situation, acknowledge the customer's right to be frustrated.

The atmosphere in your operation will be much more pleasant if each person uses both verbal and nonverbal language to treat employees and customers with mutual respect.

THOUGHT-PROVOKING QUESTIONS AND ACTION PLANS

1. How do you feel about the word *secretary*? Do you find it offensive? Why or why not?

2. Do you still call administrative assistants in your office *secretaries*? Does that impact how clients and fellow employees perceive them? What might be a better name to call them?

3. Have you ever dealt with someone who had a habit of passing the buck? How did you feel about that person? How did it impact your trust and respect for their organization?

4. Have you been trained in the right way to respond when something goes wrong? What do you say to take responsibility instead of offering excuses?

5. Think of a recent situation in which a client was unhappy because something did not happen as promised. How did you handle their complaint? Imagine responding with the AAA Train. Would that have helped resolve the situation more efficiently and diplomatically?

Being Cheap Can Cost a Lot

*People may do satisfactory work because they are forced
to. They only do superior work because they want to.*
—Dennis Kinlaw

WHEN I AM traveling to visit a new Tae Kwon Do school, I start by
looking for one thing: the number of black belts who are training at
the school. It takes a wonderful instructor to get a person to black belt level.
It takes an exceptional instructor to keep them motivated after they have
achieved the recognition.

In the business world, we should similarly be judged not by what quality of employee we get but whether or not we are capable of holding on to
them. One factor in employee retention is designing a compensation system
that motivates employees. Employees crave appreciation but they determine
how much I really appreciate them by the dollar value I put on their efforts.
If I want to attract and retain exceptional employees, I must be willing to
compensate them adequately.

For many employers, staff salaries are the biggest expense in their operation. Before a business owner hires the first employee, he must determine how to create a compensation system. Often new employers make personal sacrifices to obtain the ideal employees. A compensation system should reward employees for helping the company to achieve their goals. The employer must design a compensation system that is aligned with the business goals and creates synergy.

As a business owner, I must practice sound financial management. I am often thinking of ways to trim expenses, maximize profit, and run a lean operation. The absolute last place to be thrifty is employee salaries.

I have met employers who are greedy. I know that underpaid employees are not loyal nor do they work as hard. Underpaying employees costs too much. Scrimping on salaries may save me money short term but cost me in the long run. If I don't offer reasonable salaries my competition will. In addition, my employees will eventually not give me 100 percent effort if I take advantage of them.

My best employees will vote with their feet. They'll eventually get fed up and move on, but not before bringing down the morale and productivity of the organization. I might get away with being cheap temporarily but will have the expense of increased costs due to employee turnover.

Not every employee will choose to leave. Unfortunately my best employees are the most likely to leave. Others may elect to hang around because they "have to" or because they are too lazy to look for another job.

Just because they are still with me physically does not mean they are still with me emotionally (working at their full capacity). Worse, many harbor a resentment that can spill over into their communication with customers and fellow employees.

A business owner asked me to diagnose the cause of several negative events in his office. His business had been extremely successful at one time. Recently sales had plummeted substantially, customer retention was dropping, and he was in a panic. I did not have to investigate long before the issue became obvious.

I noticed he had an unusually high employee-turnover rate. In essence, he might as well have installed a revolving door for employees. When I questioned the turnover rate he said, "People are disposable and employee turnover is just part of running a business. It is not my fault."

Hemorrhaging employees is a big deal. It is a red flag saying something is wrong. A staff with a properly structured compensation system is a profit center, not a cost center. I reminded myself to remain open minded but was extremely skeptical. Unfortunately, employees were anxious to inform me that they were inadequately compensated. In digging deeper I discovered that salaries truly were far below the industry average.

Employees were also quick to point out that the owner had recently built a new 6,000-square-foot home. They also informed me that he purchased a new luxury car every year.

There was resentment because their salaries were low. There was much more resentment because they perceived he had adequate disposable income to change the situation. In their minds, the employees were being taken advantage of.

Employee turnover costs include the following:

- Bringing a new person onto the team requires dozens of work hours and dollars as you recruit and interview to find the right person.

- The entire team has more strain and work when an employee leaves. Other team members must take on the additional workload and add it to their already full plate until a new person is functional.

- Training new hires and bringing them up to speed is time consuming. A team member must take time away from his or her usual duties to educate the new hire. The process disrupts the normal workflow.

- Customers lose confidence in our business if there are new people serving them every time they visit. They question our leadership if we cannot hold on to employees.

- High turnover damages the momentum of the business. Healthy team dynamics requires stability. It is hard for people to really gel and come together as a cohesive unit if the team members keep changing.

The most important reason to pay your employees what they are worth is simple—it is the right thing to do. Operating from a place of integrity means we compensate fairly.

Design a performance-driven pay structure and reward the efforts of the team based on their contributions to the bottom line.

THOUGHT-PROVOKING QUESTIONS AND ACTION PLANS

1. How do the salaries in your business stack up against the industry norms? Are they lower, higher, average? Go on a recon mission, visiting other business owners, and get ballpark figures on average salaries.

2. Do your employees feel they are paid what they are worth? Do they possibly feel that you say you appreciate them but the salary you provide indicates otherwise?

3. Are your employees motivated to produce superior work because of your compensation system?

4. What is the turnover rate in your business? How do you track it so you have measurable ways to evaluate trends and compare your rate of turnover to previous years and other businesses?

5. Have you lost any quality employees because they could make better money somewhere else? In retrospect, do you wish you had seen the writing on the wall and done something differently in order to keep them on the job?

6. Have you ever been tempted to pay an employee less than she was worth because you thought you could get away with it?

Understand the
Economic Equation

If you don't make me more than you cost me, I can't keep you.
—AUTHOR UNKNOWN

A T THE AGE of twenty-six, I saw the quote above on a sign. It literally stopped me in my tracks. What an aha moment. I had been working for several years, but the economics of business had never really hit home until that moment. It had never occurred to me that if I wanted to make $50,000 a year, I had to generate more than $50,000 of revenue for my company. In fact, I had to generate a lot more or I would be a break-even, no-profit employee.

* * *

I share that epiphany with every employee. For some, the "make more than you cost" insight is often as much a shock to them as it was to me twenty years ago. For others, this is the first time an owner has taken the time to explain business economics.

In order for an employee to add to the bottom line, he needs to understand what activities generate income for the business. He also needs to have an understanding of what he could possibly do to reduce expenses. As a result of understanding this bottom-line mentality, my employees have changed. They understand that the more they stay focused on a high return on investment activity, the more money they will make. Educating the employee on the economics provides them more security and the company more stability.

Most employees want to enjoy the eight hours a day they invest in their career. They also want to perceive that their efforts are appreciated. I taught a seminar last week to a group of employees. During the question-and-answer session I was startled when an employee asked me, "How can I add value to the business I work in?"

Wow! I was blown away by this person's desire to make a difference—not just show up. She wanted to feel that she made a contribution during the time she devoted to her job. We as employers have the responsibility to make sure there is a clear understanding as to how our employees can add value.

My answer to her question was simple. I said, "Go back and ask your boss what task he would love to be able to delegate. Chances are there is something he does that he doesn't enjoy. It might be something that you would not mind handling."

We should operate under the assumption that employees want to contribute. Once employees fully understand the economics of doing business, they are more likely to focus on activities that bolster revenue.

Employees care about the bottom line if for no other reason than they realize it determines the disposable income of the business. We are obliged to create a clear vision of how to create success for employees through a stronger understanding of business economics. We must attempt to clearly communicate how each individual can add to the bottom line of the organization.

THOUGHT-PROVOKING QUESTIONS AND ACTION PLANS

1. Did anyone ever explain the economics of business to you? When and how? What impact did that have on you?

2. Do your employees understand that they each need to be a profit center?

3. Do the employees in your organization have a clear understanding of what provides economic value to the business? Do you communicate economics to potential employees prior to hire? Is it done verbally and in your employee handbook?

4. Is there anything you can do to remove activities that are not income generating? Work with employees to determine how to generate more income or cut expenses.

5. Are you personally staying focused on a high return on investment activity? What activities do you need to remove from your day to generate more income?

6. Have you ever had a situation where an employee deserved an increase in salary but the economics of the business did not allow you to provide one? How did you communicate this to the employee?

Defend Your Employees

Live so that your friends can defend you but never have to.
—ARNOLD GLASGOW

WHILE EXPERIENCING DELAYS at Chicago's O'Hare airport during a raging winter storm, we were warned that blizzard-like conditions would probably keep us from making it home to Corpus Christi, Texas. The airline personnel asked if we would prefer to stay in Chicago overnight or attempt to make it to Houston, at least partway home. We were informed that since the delays were weather related they would not be the responsibility of the airlines.

Four travelers and I opted to make it as far as we could that night. Eventually we made it to Houston only to find that we had missed our connecting flight to Corpus Christi. As we waited to retrieve our luggage, an irate customer complained to airline employees about the expense of the hotel. I was puzzled since he had been warned in advance and clearly the airlines had not created the bad weather in Chicago.

The employee continued to handle the situation graciously. She calmly explained that the airline could not provide vouchers for a hotel room since the delay was weather related. I certainly understood, as did all the other passengers. The one cranky customer would not let up.

He insisted on speaking to a manager and kept up his squeaky-wheel-gets-the-grease act. The manager on duty was called from his office. He walked into the lobby looking intimidated and defeated. He relented immediately and provided all of us with hotel vouchers. That was great for us, but how do you think that airline employee felt?

As the manager left the room to process the paperwork, the customer service representative who had originally been helping turned to a fellow employee and said under her breath, "I hate it when he makes us look bad."

Her point was understandable. She was extremely professional under the circumstances. She was again communicating and enforcing a logical company policy. Then, the manager waltzed in. He preferred to cave in to prevent dealing with the angry customer. In doing so, he made his employee look bad and he also broke the rules.

He may have made one customer happy, but he caused his employee to lose face. I wish the manager had stood up to the customer. I wanted him to defend his employee, even if it meant I would be paying for a night at the hotel.

Businesses cannot exist without customers and employees. Unfortunately, there will occasionally be challenging situations when a manager has to choose between a customer and an employee. When forced to choose I will always defend my employee and assume that she handled each situation in a competent manner.

Occasionally an employee will make a mistake. One of my employees had her first encounter with a frustrated customer about six months into the job. Eventually Mrs. Ortiz demanded to "see the owner."

After reviewing her records, it was clear that the explanation that my employee was providing was indeed incorrect. Immediately, I apologized to the customer. Instead of accepting my apology, this client demanded that I call the employee into my office. Mrs. Ortiz wanted to witness me explaining to my employee that she was right. I explained to Mrs. Ortiz, "We are having an office meeting in a few minutes. I will go over this billing with everyone in the meeting to assure that this type of error is not made again." I apologized one more time. She was not happy. Mrs. Ortiz got louder and even more insistent that I bring the employee in to be reprimanded. No matter what I said, she would not budge. For whatever reason, she was bound and determined that I undermine my staff member in her presence.

I finally said, "Mrs. Ortiz, I value your business. I refuse, however, to humiliate an employee to make you happy. Educating my employees is my responsibility and I assure you I take it very seriously. I will see that this is handled." Mrs. Ortiz looked shocked, and then seemed to understand.

It certainly would have been easier to make the customer happy, but it would have been wrong. I am accountable for the performance of my employees. I certainly would not humiliate a customer in front of my employee to make the employee happy either.

When forced to choose between supporting an employee and giving in to a customer's demands, I put myself in the employee's place. How would I want to be treated?

Create a team that you trust, then make sure they understand that you are the type of leader who will back them up. Assume competency until proven otherwise. I choose to stand up for employees when customers treat them with disrespect.

THOUGHT-PROVOKING QUESTIONS AND ACTION PLANS

1. Have you ever been in a position where a customer has demanded that you do something that is against company policy? How did you handle that situation?

2. Have you ever been overruled by a manager? What happened?

3. What is your policy about defending your employees? Can you think of a time you went to bat for an employee when a customer was out of line? What happened?

4. How do you handle the situation when a customer is right and your employee has actually made a mistake? Do your employees think you handle these situations professionally?

I Want to Be Engaged

*The first thing to realize is that employee turnover is
not an event—it is really a process of disengagement
that can take days, weeks, months, or even years until
the actual decision to leave occurs (if it ever does).*
—Leigh Branham

I KEEP A LIST of every employee who was once employed by our company.
Beside each name is my perception of the reason they decided to leave or
were let go. The list is titled "Who didn't work out—why??"

Remember, people don't quit jobs; they quit managers. I am either energizing employees or sucking the life out of them.

In studying the causes of my employee turnover, I see several common
characteristics. Perhaps most significantly, I recognize that there was a disengagement process in each and every case. I was able to sense that something was amiss with either the individual or the dynamics of the team. I
now realize that it is much easier to catch a problem early than it is to deal
with damage once the situation gets out of control.

Think back to a job that you did not enjoy. In each job that I left there was a defining moment or specific reason that I left. I never left because I was bored or just wanted more money. Unfortunately we now live in a society where employees almost expect that they will not be pleased with their job long term. Seldom do employees seem to be surprised when a negative event causes them to be disenchanted with their job. The employee may feel an employer expects her to prioritize the job over family or may feel the employer micromanages employees.

One employer I worked for promised a raise at a specific time. Initially I was patient when the allotted time came and went. Several months later, I had lost my patience. Not only was there no raise but there was not even a discussion to explain the change in plans. I finally approached the manager who had promised the raise and was told that there would be no raise. She indicated that I must be "confused" as to what had been promised. Trust was immediately shattered.

Leigh Branham's book *The 7 Hidden Reasons Employees Leave* does a wonderful job of explaining the disengagement process that employees go through when they are disenchanted. As employers we need to understand the warning signs that become obvious if we are willing to see them. We are also responsible for stopping the process of disengagement.

The specific reasons why employees did not work out in my office are the following:

- Personal problems. An employee with habitual turmoil in his personal life will eventually allow it to interfere with his ability to get the job done. A person with excessive relationship issues or major financial issues may have trouble focusing over time.

- Maverick. Some people are focused primarily on their own personal gain. A successful business needs team members who also have a tremendous focus on creating success for the team.

- Drama queens/kings. Some employees thrive on creating intense conflict. Whether problems need to be fixed or fights break out, these employees add stress.

- Bums. There are actually people who are inherently lazy. It is impossible to create a team atmosphere when a team member chooses to be motivationally challenged.

- Intelligence. Unfortunately I have worked with people who were really nice but were incapable of learning the information required to do the job. This is certainly the most difficult situation—when the heart is there but the ability is lacking to handle the issues that may arise.

- Mommy syndrome. Life roles change and there are times when a person will struggle with whether they belong in the working world or at home raising children. There is absolutely nothing wrong with deciding to stay at home.

On the other hand, every employee who has worked well shares specific characteristics:

- Accommodating. They are easy to get along with and eager to please.

- Self-structured. They are organized, focused, and self-disciplined.

- Team players. They understand that individual success with team failure equals failure.

Several years ago there existed a market condition that was going to have a significant negative impact on our business. As I made my employees aware of the situation, I saw the panic arise. I explained the circumstances and then was quiet for a few seconds to allow the information to sink in. After a few seconds I saw each of the employees relax. They were each going through a mental process that was almost visible. I could see them thinking, "How is this going to impact me personally?"

Each of these employees had been with me for years. They had been through several negative events. They had experienced obstacles and knew we would survive. Every employee deduced within seconds that we would be OK—except Theresa. Theresa never said a word but I could see in her face that she was really concerned. I could have assumed she would eventually be OK. I could have let it go.

This was a defining moment. I knew if I ignored her discomfort she may have become disengaged. I understood that it was important that we continue to communicate until we were again all on the same page.

As everyone watched, I talked the group down memory lane. I reminded them of how difficult the market had been in 1994 and 2000. We talked about how the stress level eventually went back to normal. I explained that this was just the next challenge.

Theresa's stress level gradually diminished but she still had some concern. Finally I got to the point. I said, "Theresa, repeat after me. 'Laura, I trust you.'" She never took her eyes off me as she quietly said, "Laura I trust you."

I responded with "That was not convincing. Say it again. 'Laura, I trust you.'"

Eventually calm returned to her face and she said with conviction, "Laura, I trust you."

In order to keep the process of disengagement from moving forward I had to

- Handle the situation immediately,
- Acknowledge there was a challenge,
- Communicate that I understood her concern, and
- Follow up to make sure the trust was truly rebuilt.

Being able to instinctively determine that an employee has become disengaged requires intuition. It also requires consistent communication with employees. I am convinced that employees want to communicate when they have a defining moment that causes them to become disengaged. They would prefer not to become disengaged. Employees do not want to leave their current job. They want to have resolution to the issues that cause discomfort.

It is much easier to ignore the warning signs when a staff member becomes disengaged. It is my job to be intuitive enough to know when we are no longer working together toward the company goals. I also have to be willing to deal with the situation if it arises.

Keeping open communications and providing clear direction radically reduces the chances that an employee will become disengaged. Stay conscious of the engagement level of each employee and tackle issues quickly.

THOUGHT-PROVOKING QUESTIONS AND ACTION PLANS

1. Have you ever become disenchanted with a job and tried to work with your employer to resolve the situation? What were the results?

2. What characteristics have you found that caused colleagues to not work well within a team?

3. Are you sure that everyone in your current operation is fully engaged and committed to the organization? If not, how will you begin the communication process to provide resolution?

4. Make a list of each employee who did not work out in your organization. Write beside each name the characteristic that caused that person not to be a permanent part of the organization.

5. Make a list of the colleagues in your current operation. What positive characteristics do these employees have in common?

6. Do you currently have disengaged employees? Do you wonder if they are working when you are not watching?

Three Strikes—You're Out

*If you aren't fired with enthusiasm, you
will be fired with enthusiasm.*
—Vince Lombardi

I F WE FAIL to take action when an employee is slacking off, we fail the team. Morale and productivity will quickly suffer because employees deduce, "So-and-so is falling down on the job and no one cares. Why should I put in extra effort when she is getting away with slacking off?"

Do you want to know how I took the trauma out of termination? I found a way to take the personal out of it. I establish measurable expectations *prior* to hiring. These standards and expectations are defined in our employee handbook. Potential employees are required to read them before their first interview.

With an employee handbook defining the basic rules and quantifiable expectations, behavior is less subjective. I simply point to the policy in our handbook that clearly outlines our work standards. In the event an employee is underperforming, I meet with that person in private and point out exactly how and why her work behavior is unsatisfactory. There is no guesswork or surprise. I do not send subtle signals that I am unhappy with her work, and the employee does not have to read between the lines.

If an employee is not meeting expectations I need to see if there is an outside situation contributing to the lackluster performance (an issue in his personal life, etc.). I have to determine whether or not there may be a condition in the office that is somehow causing him to perform poorly.

After a frank conversation, the ball is in the employee's court. The success or failure of each employee is her choice and responsibility. I am no longer traumatized if I have to terminate an employee. I am very careful to set clear expectations upfront, provide coaching along the way, and give the employee every chance to do what is needed to remain as part of the team.

I recently flew into the Dallas–Fort Worth airport to attend a meeting. As I approached the animated person behind the rental car counter, I knew I was in for an interesting experience. The attendant was communicating her frustrations to someone on the phone. I tried to stay in a good mood while I patiently waited and listened to what was obviously a personal conversation. As an employer, my first thought was *I wish she was not doing this on company time.* My mood changed instantly as she slammed down the phone and declared, "I hate Texans . . ." Those are fighting words.

I know she said something after the word "Texan" but my mind shut down immediately. She proceeded to inform me that her electricity had been cut off and she hated living in Texas. Her behavior was completely inappropriate.

My work entails me traveling frequently and I see many examples of bad service. My immediate reaction is simple—if you were my employee . . .

Occasionally there are circumstances where I feel that my employees could have handled a situation better. I know without a doubt that my customers would never have to deal with behavior that far out of line. Several years ago I hired someone and two customers complained about her behavior within her first sixty days on the job. They both used the exact same words in describing her behavior. They said she was "rude and sarcastic."

After the first incident my employee and I spent time talking about how to appropriately handle a difficult situation. I acknowledged that the customer could have been out of line and reinforced our company philosophy of zero tolerance for disrespectful treatment of customers.

When the second call came in the conversation was less pleasant. My exact words were, "Working here is like playing baseball. You now have two strikes. If I ever have another customer call to complain that you were rude, you will be terminated immediately. Your boss (the office manager) has been here six years and I have *never* had a customer call to complain about her attitude."

After a conversation like this, one of two things happens:

- The employee immediately changes her behavior. Once employees know that rudeness will not be tolerated and see how they are being perceived by others, they shape up.

- The employee does not change her behavior. This rarely happens. If an employee chooses to continue to break our rules, our next conversation will probably be an exit interview.

The three-strike process is simple.

- Strike one. Assume that the customer could have been out of line and communicate the appropriate way to handle the situation.

- Strike two. Explain that the repeated behavior is unacceptable. Request that the employee sign paperwork acknowledging the infraction. Include in the paperwork language that makes it clear that this type of infraction could cause the job to be in jeopardy.

- Strike three. They are out!

Being rude is a choice. Being rude does not happen accidentally. I genuinely love every person I work with. I am determined to enjoy coming to work, and each person who works in our office should enjoy the same luxury.

There are extenuating circumstances when the three-strike rule does not come into play. An employee would be terminated immediately if there are ethics issues such as stolen money or in the event that an employee's behavior was deemed to possibly endanger fellow employees or customers (e.g., violent behavior, discovery of firearms). I personally always contact an attorney in the event that I have to terminate an employee without going through a progressive disciplinary program. If I am ever unclear in regards to whether or not a termination is legal, I always contact an attorney.

You can often prevent negative experiences within your organization by setting clear expectations and modeling the behavior that you desire.

Unfortunately there will be times when education or correction is necessary. I choose to have a progressive disciplinary system that deals with less than stellar performance immediately.

THOUGHT-PROVOKING QUESTIONS AND ACTION PLANS

1. Are your employees enthusiastic and hardworking? Do they treat the business like it is their own?

2. Are expectations that treating fellow employees or customers disrespectfully will not be tolerated set prior to employment?

3. What would you do if an employee spoke disrespectfully to a fellow employee or customer? Do you allow employee dissention?

4. How do you determine who was really at fault when there is a dispute between employees? How would you hold that person accountable?

5. Are you comfortable with the conversation that is necessary when termination is inevitable? What can you do to take the personal out of it?

Shoot Your Own Horse

One of the toughest things to learn is the ability to make yourself do the thing you have to do, when it ought to be done, whether you like it or not.
—Thomas Henry Huxley

THE MOST DIFFICULT part of being self-employed is terminating an employee. When termination becomes inevitable, there is a mixture of relief and stress. It is always sad because most of us do not enjoy hurting people. Even if he or she hates the job, it is never pleasant to explain to someone that things are not working out. The "I am letting you go" conversations can turn ugly. I had one employee argue with me during the termination, as if it was open for discussion.

The first time I had to terminate someone, I literally cried for three days prior to "doing the deed." I was crushed at the thought of having to let someone go. I agonized over how this was going to affect her. I could not sleep at night because I kept going over and over in my head how I could deliver the news in as painless a way as possible. Imagine my surprise when the employee looked completely nonchalant. I was traumatized, but to her it was no big deal (which is a big clue as to why she was not working out).

Although terminating an employee is completely unpleasant, I have learned not to avoid it. Once the process is inevitable I have learned the proper way to handle things:

- Don't hesitate. Once the decision has been made, move quickly. I saw Harvey Mackay speak at a National Speakers Association convention and will always remember a particular line he described as his biggest lesson learned. He said, "It is not the people I have fired that have caused me problems. It is the people I should have fired and didn't."

- Handle it personally. Termination of an employee is a task that is always handled by me. In the Wild West there was a code of honor that dictated men take care of their own dirty work. If a horse was injured and had to be put down, the owner would take responsibility. It was unpleasant but it was a cowboy's way of showing respect to his companion. There are some things you do not delegate—this is one of them.

If I have to terminate someone, I must admit I probably did not hire the right person in the first place. Ouch! If I did hire the right person and things did not work out then I may not have provided the education and coaching that was needed. In either case, it sure feels like I have failed as a leader.

Do everything in your power to make each situation with an employee work. If termination is inevitable, handle the situation personally and allow the person to leave with their self-respect intact. One thing is for sure—it is never good to hold on to a non-performer for too long.

THOUGHT-PROVOKING QUESTIONS AND ACTION PLANS

1. Have you ever had to terminate an employee? How did you handle it?

2. Would you say you are conflict averse? Can you think of a time you should have let an employee go and you did not, or you delayed because you dreaded the confrontation? What happened?

3. Is an employee on your team underperforming? How is that individual's work behavior unsatisfactory? Have you exhausted all opportunities to improve the situation?

4. How and when are you going to meet with that employee and hold him accountable for his behavior? What are you going to say?

5. If that staff member chooses to continue to break your rules or not perform to standard, how are you going to let her go?

Feedback Without Fear

No matter how much you disagree with your kin,
if you are a thoroughbred you will not discuss
their shortcomings with the neighbors.
—Tom Thompson

I LEARNED A LOT in the thirteen years I worked for others. One thing I learned was how consistently unpleasant most performance reviews are. One co-worker said (only half-kidding) she would rather be shot than subject herself to being raked over the coals again. Performance appraisals should not cause trepidation.

It is in everyone's best interest for a company to have performance appraisals. The process allows both employers and employees to know where they stand. Employers need to design a system to openly discuss performance. A well-designed performance appraisal system will provide career clarity and improve satisfaction for employees.

The following are keys to a positive review process.

- Have performance appraisals sporadically, not at a prescribed time. I worked for a firm that conducted performance reviews every April. Knowing exactly when you would be evaluated had a bizarre effect. In March and April of every year, paranoia was off the charts. Then, once the performance appraisal was over, everyone slacked off.

- Never drop a bomb during a performance appraisal. We should not save the bad stuff. Who wants to hear "Do you remember in August of last year when you . . . ?" If an employee does something wrong, he or she should know it immediately. Although the timing of the reviews is unpredictable, the content should never be a surprise. The strengths and weaknesses discussed during the performance review should also be discussed during daily interaction. Frequent informal conversations can drastically reduce the stress level.

- Provide potential employees with a copy of the performance review form prior to their taking the job. You will shock future employees when you explain what your specific expectations are in advance. They will appreciate understanding clearly what types of behaviors are expected and what criteria they will be measured on. Some may actually opt out of the job. If they are not willing to be on time, follow office procedures, and meet production requirements, you are better off finding out prior to their taking the job. We include this information in our employee handbook and obtain an employee's signature of agreement at the time of hire.

- Never tie performance reviews to salary increases. If getting a raise is dependent on receiving a positive evaluation, employees will not be receptive to anything but positive communications. They will aggressively defend any less-than-stellar feedback. It may be perceived that deficiencies in an employee's performance could jeopardize a possible pay increase. The performance review will turn into a debate instead of an honest discussion.

- Provide balanced information on compliments and concerns. There should be at least three to five positive communications for every negative one. The purpose is to give constructive feedback so employees have an accurate idea of how they are performing and are motivated to do better.

- Make sure discussions regarding weaknesses of employees stay between the employer and that employee. Employees should trust that if you are unhappy with an employee's performance, you will discuss the shortcoming with them and no one else.

At least once a year I sit down with each employee individually and have a reverse performance review. One day a manager I worked for teasingly asked, "OK, it is time for performance reviews. Do you want to review me or should I review you?" This was an employer whom I adored and I trusted he had not come in for a surprise attack. The more I thought about what he said, the more I liked the idea. What a great concept. Why not let employees give me a performance review? We informally discuss how I could better lead the team. I ask what they would do differently if they were running the business. I find out whether or not the job is living up to their expectations. Am I delivering what I promised? Finally, we talk about how I can help them be more successful in their job.

Reverse performance reviews will often uncover a defining moment that has caused an employee to become partially disengaged. Make sure that the employee feels comfortable that you will discuss his weaknesses with him only. He should also be able to trust that you will not go back to the team with any negative information that is discussed during the reverse performance review.

Ken Blanchard says, "Feedback is the breakfast of champions." Performance reviews do not have to be painful—feedback can actually improve focus.

THOUGHT-PROVOKING QUESTIONS AND ACTION PLANS

1. How often do you have performance reviews in your business? Are they scheduled at regular intervals? How does that affect the team's morale and effectiveness?

2. Have you ever been the victim of a traumatic performance evaluation? How did that impact you?

3. Do you provide feedback that includes a reasonable amount of positive comments in addition to the areas that require improvement?

4. Do you confirm with employees that you are fully enabling them to achieve their individual goals? What tools or training could you provide to improve their success?

5. Have you ever allowed your employees to give you a performance review? Why or why not?

Part 4
DEVIL'S IN THE DETAILS

Sixty Days to Sanity

You cannot help men permanently by doing for them
what they could and should do for themselves.
—ABRAHAM LINCOLN

ONCE I HAVE become an autopilot leader, done my upfront alignment, and placed the right team in position, it is time to tend to the details. I need to make sure the entire team is empowered to assist in moving the organization toward its goals. It is my job to see to it that the answers to any questions that may come their way are at their fingertips.

I once decided that for the next sixty days, I would stop every time an employee asked a question and determine, "Does the answer to this question already exist in writing? If it does, do all employees know where to find it?"

Staff correlates sharing of information with trust. As I provide crucial information to employees I am communicating that I deem them to be integral in propelling the business toward our goals. I need to teach employees where to find answers and how to analyze and best handle each situation.

Knowledgeable employees are more effective workers. In my original business model, the business revolved around me. I unintentionally became an information hog. It may have pumped up my ego but unknowingly I was undermining my employees' effectiveness. Instead of developing them, I was forcing them to be dependent on me.

It became my goal to create a resource with every policy, procedure, and practice so staff members were able to make their own decisions instead of having to request help from me or another employee. Giving them access to everything they needed also gave them the opportunity and obligation to be self-sufficient.

When this process began we found that some things that should have been defined in writing were not. In addition, we had to be determined to require that employees be accountable for learning where to find the answers.

Some employees were taking the lazy way out by simply soliciting a quick answer from a colleague. That behavior was easier than researching the answer but not very effective for the team. This perpetuated what one staff member called "self-induced ignorance."

We eventually instituted a new rule: Prior to asking a question of anyone, you have to research the answer first. We have to hold each other accountable for being self-sufficient autonomous adults. When a person comes to me with a question that we know is defined in writing, I will often sarcastically remark, "Oh, do you need me to read to you?" The comment was always made in jest. It didn't take long for everyone to get into the habit of looking for the answers before asking questions. This additional training caused a noticeable boost in the confidence level of the team.

Employees are encouraged to ask questions if they do not understand a policy or procedure after they have looked it up. I do not want them to be afraid to ask a question if they have truly done their research. Of course, there is nothing wrong with an employee saying, "I have researched this question and my interpretation of the correct answer is . . . I just want to verify this with you." I will gladly reassure them that they have come to the right conclusion.

The entire process is used to remind employees that they are as capable of making sound decisions as I am. It also reinforces the perspective that laziness is not tolerated. You may be thinking, "Aren't there exceptions?

Aren't there unusual circumstances that are so rare they are not covered in writing?" Of course there are but they are very few.

It is amazing how much time there is to handle those rare exceptions when the day-to-day operations are handled with confidence by all involved. Create autonomous employees who feel comfortable handling any situation.

THOUGHT-PROVOKING QUESTIONS AND ACTION PLANS

1. For the next sixty days, every time someone asks you a question, stop and think: Does the answer exist in writing? If yes, show them where to find the answer. If not, define it in writing and make sure everyone knows where the answer is. You do not need to be the office encyclopedia. Do not show them the answers; teach them to think on their own.

2. Do you have information-hog tendencies? Do you enjoy being the person who others come to for information? How does that affect the people around you?

3. How do you hold employees accountable for finding their own answers instead of supplying answers for them?

4. Have you defined and saved electronically all relevant information that your team might need? If not, explain precisely how you are going to get this project started this week.

5. Are you the person in the office who is constantly interrupting others with questions? Hold yourself accountable. For the next sixty days, each time you come up with a question to which you do not know the answer, ask your staff to show you where to find the answer in writing. Try never to ask the same question again.

Remember Why We Do This

My mother said to me, "If you become a soldier, you'll be a general; if you become a monk, you'll end up as the pope." Instead I became a painter and wound up as Picasso.
—PABLO PICASSO

M OST OF US grow up with the realization that someday we will have to choose a career. Some children are fortunate enough to know at an early age that they want to be a fireman, an astronaut, or a teacher. For the rest of us, it takes a little or a lot longer. Believe it or not, my career in insurance was originally chosen by default. My grandfather and my mother were both in insurance. I initially saw this industry simply as a known way to make a living.

When I graduated from college I knew it was a good time to make a conscious decision as to what career I was going to pursue. As I thought about the many options I realized I really enjoyed the industry I was already in. Not long afterward, I opened my own office. One of the first insurance reviews I did was the most memorable.

Josephine stopped me as I went through my usual list of questions. She said, "Do you mind if I tell you a story?" I had been so busy going through my routine checklist that I was a little taken aback. I stopped writing, put down my pen, and said, "Please do."

Josephine said, "Several years ago my husband and I reviewed our insurance with our agent. During the process the agent brought to our attention that we did not have enough life insurance to pay off our mortgage in the event of death. The agent encouraged us to solve the problem immediately but we chose not to do anything at that time.

"After thinking about it for a while, my husband and I decided this was too important to ignore. He called our agent and told him we wanted to buy the coverage after all. The agent told him, 'I'm going hunting tomorrow and will be gone for two weeks. Can we set up an appointment to handle that when I get back?'

"My husband and I were in no rush. An appointment was scheduled for later that month." Josephine paused for a moment and then said quietly, "One week later my husband died unexpectedly. He had an aneurysm but we didn't know it."

She went on to explain that the agent showed up to the funeral in tears because he knew that Josephine had children at home and did not have resources to replace her husband's income.

I was shocked. I sat speechless. Moments later I was flooded with a newfound sense of the importance and responsibility for what I do. I immediately made the transition from a transaction mentality and became conscious of the impact we have on others.

From that moment on I no longer considered my job simply as a way of making ends meet. I realized that the decisions my employees and I make can affect people's lives drastically. When I find myself robotically going through the motions, I go back to that experience many years ago.

We stop and think about the true value our business has to others. To paraphrase Maurice Sendak, there is more to our job than getting a paycheck. We must focus on the importance of our behaviors and how they impact others.

THOUGHT-PROVOKING QUESTIONS AND ACTION PLANS

1. Did you proactively choose to work in the industry you are currently in? Do you take pride in your performance at work?

2. Be honest. Do you sometimes find yourself going through the motions with your clients? Are you so familiar with some scripts that you become robotic during the sales process?

3. How can you remind yourself on a daily basis that you have an impact on your clients? What is needed to make sure that employees remain conscious of the responsibilities they have?

4. Are you able to stay focused on the clients' needs instead of thinking about the commissions or revenues that would be produced? Create a client-focused culture and the sales will take care of themselves. Write down how you will begin this process and share it with your staff.

Make a Difference

A business that makes nothing but money is a poor business.
—HENRY FORD

IF YOU ARE reading this book, I would dare say that you understand what it feels like to be overwhelmed. You may perceive yourself to be too busy to make a difference in the world. At times our natural tendency is to become engrossed in our self-discovery and improving our personal situation. Life is so much richer when we focus on how we can have a positive impact on those around us. I hope each of you has a personal conviction to be involved in the community and make a difference.

It is easy to sit back and feel that individually we will not be able to have a substantial impact on society. Individuals like Martin Luther King, Mother Teresa, and so many others have made a tremendous impact because of their focused determination to make a difference. Life is not a spectator sport. Woodrow Wilson said, "You are here to enrich the world, and you impoverish yourself if you forget the errand."

How can you be a catalyst for change in our world or your community? First, realize that your primary responsibility is to have an impact on your family. I feel so blessed to have grown up in a loving family. I still have the baseball glove that my dad used to play softball with me over thirty years ago. I have also kept the Christmas ornaments and Barbie doll clothes that my mother and I made as a child. Cherish the time you have with your family and create traditions and rituals that they will recall fondly years from now.

Second, choose to have a positive impact on those whom you come in contact with naturally. We have the ability to serve others in our daily walk. Help a friend who has had surgery. Offer a ride to someone without a vehicle. Take care of a friend's child so she can have a night off. Show a genuine interest in a customer who appears to be having a bad day. Little things mean a lot.

Finally, decide to have an impact on the local community and beyond. Do not feel obligated to get involved with every good cause. Determine where there is a need in the community that you are passionate about. You may be touched by the needs of the homeless, the elderly, or victims of domestic violence. My experiences have determined which causes I care most about. It is best for me to spend my time and donate money in those areas.

Is your group involved in community projects? Perhaps you can work together as a team to raise funds for a community playground or help serve a Thanksgiving dinner for the homeless. Become involved in projects that are already in motion. Include your children and the children of your employees where appropriate. Instill in the next generation the need to give back.

I am much more well-rounded when making money is not my primary objective. Life is genuinely enriched when it revolves around helping others get ahead. The true depth of a person's character is how willing he or she is to do something that may never be acknowledged by others or even known by the person who benefits. Seek out opportunities to positively impact persons in your community and beyond.

THOUGHT-PROVOKING QUESTIONS AND ACTION PLANS

1. What group are you passionate about helping? How can you get involved?

2. Who has helped you mature and grow in the past? Have you thanked them for the contribution they made to your life?

3. What projects could you become involved with that could include your children? How can you use that experience to teach your children the importance of giving back to society?

4. Does your company collectively get involved in giving back to the community? Does that experience benefit your business? How?

Operating in a Silo

It is not enough to be busy. Ants are busy.
The question is, "What are you busy at?"
—Mark Twain

Businesses ultimately have two major goals—providing a great product or service for consumers and providing enjoyable employment and financial opportunities for the employer and employees. Losing sight of either goal can be detrimental to the long-term success of a business.

Businesses must be viewed holistically. The vision and overall mentality of the business must consider how each decision will impact the entire organization, not just one department. We cannot engage in an action in one area that may cause a dysfunction in another area.

Put every decision inside of the business through a funnel:

- Is what we are contemplating beneficial for the company in both the short term and the long term?

- Is what we are contemplating favorable for the employees as a team? Will it improve morale and encourage teamwork?

- Is the contemplated change advantageous for employees individually? Will it be profitable financially for the company as well as for individual employees?

- Is the contemplated change going to improve one critical variable but cause disproportionate damage in another area?

- Is the contemplated change being communicated horizontally through all levels of the organization?

- Is the contemplated move going to improve customer loyalty for the ideal client? I say *ideal client* for a reason. It is impossible to make everyone happy. Would the customers who positively impact the bottom line vote for the change you are considering?

Positive action in one area can cause dysfunction in another area. I can implement a process that would drive in a disproportionate amount of "less than ideal" customers. This may increase my customers but not necessarily add to the bottom line long term.

Reward systems and processes need to be aligned to be mutually beneficial for the customer, investors, employees, and business owner. The proposed change needs to be good for all involved both short and long term, and it must propel the organization toward established goals. Consider the impact decisions will have horizontally and vertically in the company.

THOUGHT-PROVOKING QUESTIONS AND ACTION PLANS

1. Think of a marketing program that your business is contemplating. Does it pass the funnel test?

2. What is the financial impact of the decision the company is contemplating?

3. Does your business provide a highly cooperative environment? Does a mentality of abundance exist or is there a sense of scarcity?

4. Are any of your departments allowed to focus inward and operate without considering how their behaviors may impact other departments in the organization?

We Have to Start
Meeting Like This

We are going to continue having these meetings,
everyday, until I find out why no work is getting done.
—QUOTE FROM A CORPORATE MEETING

WOULD YOUR EMPLOYEES attend your meetings if they were not mandatory? Do they see true value in the time invested? We have all been in insanely boring meetings where leaders seem to feel a need to justify their existence by communicating a tremendous amount of irrelevant information.

Millions of meetings take place in the United States every day. Meetings are designed to increase production and office efficiency. They can do exactly the opposite and many participants would say that often meeting time is wasted. Attending unproductive meetings can reduce the time available to sell or service customers.

Weekly feedback should not be optional. Good employees crave the education and feedback that regular meetings can provide. I prefer to schedule meetings during business hours. I do not want employees to resent having to come in early or stay late, even if they are getting paid. We either forward our phones to another office or have a part-time employee answer calls while we are in the meeting.

Ideally office meetings have an agenda. Winging it doesn't show respect for the attendees' time. Employees can be responsible for portions of the office meeting. When you rotate leadership it develops skills. This empowers and educates employees simultaneously. It also means we all look forward to our meetings because each one is different. Instead of being the same old same old, each employee brings his or her unique style to the table.

During our meetings, we

- Review progress on our measurable business goals for the company and for individuals;
- Discuss specific markets and/or promotions;
- Train on a new procedure or review previous training; and
- Share a success story in order to focus on our achievements.

On occasion we will invite an outsider to make a presentation during our meeting. A vendor or someone from a complementary industry could add a unique prospective to our organization.

Are you thinking, "We do not have time for meetings"? With appropriate planning, meetings can actually save time and money. They prevent frustration and possible mistakes by providing proper training. They eliminate costly errors that occur when employees are not aware of changes.

Keys to a successful meeting include the following:

- Create handouts in advance. Expecting participants to take notes leads to less listening and more anxiety.
- Talk less, do more. Make sure the meeting is interactive instead of being a lecture.
- Break down your information. The more steps you create in the learning process, the better.
- Stick to the scheduled time frame. Meetings that drag on are painful to everyone.
- Include feedback on success through measurement of critical variables.

Office meetings can increase enthusiasm if conducted properly. As an employer, strive to create meetings that the team would choose to attend even if they did not have to. Meet on a regular basis to make sure the team is accomplishing goals.

THOUGHT-PROVOKING QUESTIONS AND ACTION PLANS

1. Do you have regularly scheduled office meetings?

2. How would your employees describe your meetings? Would they consider them time well spent?

3. What is one specific step you can take to run office meetings that contribute to everyone's job performance and sense of team spirit?

4. Do you bring production and retention numbers to office meetings so that everyone has a clear picture of how the team is doing?

5. Who could you bring in to speak at an office meeting to provide insight for your team?

Confidence Transfer

Confidence is the foundation for all business relations.
The degree of confidence a man has in others, and the
degree of confidence others have in him, determines a
man's standing in the commercial and industrial world.
—WILLIAM J. H. BOETCKE

M Y LEVEL OF success in business will be radically impacted by my ability to develop relationships. Associates and customers must have confidence in my integrity and competence. My ability to transfer the confidence that the consumer and associates have in me to others can work as an accelerant to increase the natural process of growth. If I cannot transfer the confidence that a customer has in me to my associates, we will have limited growth.

Occasionally, an entrepreneur tells me, "I want to know all my customers." This is a noble concept and there is certainly nothing wrong as long as that business owner understands the trade-off. I am only one person and cannot impact as many people as the entire team can.

If I want every customer to be able to speak to me personally then I must accept that I am putting a cap on potential growth. There are limitations to what one person can accomplish. As business owners we must balance the desire of certain clients to personally communicate with the owner and our desire to grow the business by leveraging employees.

Create a business where the customer gains confidence in the entire team with their first interaction. We try very hard to conduct most applications in person. It is difficult to build a long-term relationship unless someone within the organization is face to face with a customer.

Regardless of whom the new customer is dealing with, we attempt to educate the customer, close the deal, and transfer the confidence he has throughout the organization.

The new customer needs to be confident that the business owner appreciates their business and that everyone in the organization is capable from day one. If I close the deal, I make sure the customer meets my associates so I can transfer the confidence they have in me to others.

I meet as many new customers as possible, but I am not always the person whom a prospect deals with initially. If an associate takes care of a new client, then the customer has confidence in that associate. I need to have the employee transfer that confidence to me.

I'll go to the associate's desk to meet a new customer so I can communicate to the client that I personally appreciate his or her business. I then make sure that the customer is confident enough in everyone in the office so that he is not insistent on speaking only to me or to his original contact.

After talking to the new client for a few minutes, I thank her for entrusting her business to us. Then I tell her, "I am sure Stacy (I use the name of their insurance advisor) explained to you that everyone in the office is fully licensed. Either of us would be glad to help you. If she or I are on the phone when you call, I assure you that the person who answers the call will drop everything and take care of you immediately."

Communicating this promise to our new clients produces several benefits. Clients feel reassured that their needs will be handled even if the person they originally dealt with is not available. This also reduces potential frustration because clients know they do not have to wait for any particular person because he is the only capable person. The person that answers the call owns the issue.

There is an added benefit for staff—they are better able to control their time because customers are not insisting on talking to the person who originally sold them the policy.

Furthermore, this promotes customer loyalty to our business versus loyalty to a specific employee. In the event of employee turnover, we do not alienate or lose a client who has become attached to a specific employee.

This education is an ongoing process. If a client insists on speaking to me, I do the following:

- I handle their request. My primary concern is that they know we will be there for them. If I tell them I am busy and transfer the call to another employee, they will assume I do not consider them important.

- Once I have handled their requested action, I wrap up the conversation by saying, "I know you had to wait for me. I am not sure if I have introduced you to Lori. She is the staff member who answered the phone. She is fully licensed, as is every person in our office. The next time you call, if I am on the phone or out of the office, please know that whoever you are speaking to will be glad to take care of you immediately."

Since I do not take care of every client, I am available for people who need me most. If a client has a major issue or is panicked at the scene of an accident, I am available.

The crucial part of this process is ensuring that the customer understands that we have a team of leaders. The team cares about his/her needs and will see to it that he/she is completely satisfied.

Keep in mind—I make promises. I promise that I have capable staff and that we will immediately take care of customers. One negative experience and I have blown it. It is crucial that I make sure we live up to the promises. I need the customer to feel confident with every contact regardless of the experience level or position of the person she is dealing with. Transfer the confidence that consumers have throughout the organization.

THOUGHT-PROVOKING QUESTIONS AND ACTION PLANS

1. Do you have a policy about personally introducing yourself to new clients? What is that? What type of statement does that make to new clients?

2. Do you have a system for communicating to clients that *anyone* in the office is capable of helping them, not just the business owner? What is that?

3. Have you had a client insist on dealing only with you? How did you handle that?

4. Do you have customers who have confidence in your employees but not in you? How will you change the dynamics so they feel confident even if they cannot get to their "favorite" person?

5. What ways can your business transfer confidence that the customer has in one team member to other team members?

Zap Your UPOs

Organization is what you do before you do it,
so when you do it, it doesn't get all messed up.
—Winnie the Pooh

THE CUSTOMER'S FIRST impression is often a lasting one. I need to be very conscious of what a customer's first impression of our operation will be.

In our operation, the first impression often begins on the phone. Is the phone consistently answered in a professional manner? Are prospects and customers taken care of immediately? Is there something about our business that differentiates us from the competition? If I am not able to show that we are unique in some way, the consumer often will shop on price alone. The impression we make determines our success.

The physical appearance of the business plays a key determinant in the impression we make on clients. How did we decide where to put the business? Do customers walk in and see UPOs (unidentified piled objects) all over the place?

Customers have already made a lot of assumptions about our business once they see the location and walk in the door. First impressions determine whether clients consider us professionals. Their initial perceptions create a reality you will have a difficult time overcoming.

We have all heard the most important determinant for retail success is "location, location, location." Should I choose to be in a high-traffic location or would an office complex be a better decision? There are advantages and disadvantages to each, depending on what type of business you operate. In some businesses high traffic is an advantage, in others it's a major inconvenience.

Once the decision was made as to where I would locate the business, we had to decide how to furnish it. I was visiting an office several years ago and overheard a client say in disgust, "No wonder my prices are so high. Look at all this fancy furniture." That client believed that the owner was inflating rates in order to pay for his opulent office. I decided I wanted my office to look classy and professional but not ostentatious or pretentious.

Next I had to consider the physical layout of the furniture. I wanted it to look clean, organized, and professional. I want employees to have enough privacy to keep them from feeling claustrophobic but not be so distant from each other that they would be less likely to assist others. Remember that privacy is a luxury that seldom furthers organizational goals.

A client's perception of whether or not your desk is organized plays a huge role in the overall professional impression of your business. If clients walk into my office and see cluttered chaos, what will they think? If they see desks overflowing with UPOs, they will probably worry about whether I will be capable of handling their immediate needs when a crisis develops.

If they see desks stacked high with assorted files and unanswered phone messages, they are probably concerned their paperwork will get lost. In all likelihood, they are concluding, "If they are this sloppy in their work habits, how can I trust them?"

You have heard the old proverb "A place for everything and everything in its place." We believe in following that adage because it saves countless hours looking for misplaced items. In our office, we have a systemized way to organize every space.

Every desk in our office is identically organized. Envelopes go in the top-right drawer. Tape, scissors, and extra pens are always in the middle drawer under the computer. This may seem trivial, but it means no wasted time, no wasted energy, and no unnecessary stress.

This system allows for consistency. The physical location of paperwork on the desk also indicates at what stage a particular file is in the process flow. The location on the desk indicates what is to be done next. If a file is in the top of my two-drawer file cabinet then everyone knows it's a hot lead. There will be a note on the folder indicating what we are waiting for. If a file is in my top-left drawer, that indicates that I have work that is not complete. Again, the location of the work indicates its stage.

Furthermore, if an employee is out of the office and a customer calls with a question, another employee can quickly locate the pertinent paperwork. It is very easy for one employee to confidently pick up where another has left off. Paper has been eliminated whenever possible. All relevant information is stored electronically. Messages are sent electronically, not written on paper.

I was consulting with a business and the office manager confided to me, "I am so glad you are finally here. The owner has been making us clean the office for two weeks because you were coming!" How crazy is that? The owner didn't organize his office for the customers but did organize it for me. Ultimately customers pay our salaries. It is much more important to impress clients than consultants.

Here is a good rule of thumb. Ask yourself, "What VIP or celebrity would I love to meet?" For me it would be Jon Bon Jovi, Joyce Meyer, or John Maxwell (I have diverse interests). I frequently ask myself, "If that person gave me five minutes' notice for an impromptu visit, would we need to drop everything and run around cleaning?"

If so, it is time to get busy now.

Hopefully, everyone who walks into my office is treated as a VIP. Hopefully, my business is aesthetically pleasing at all times, not just when someone special pays a visit.

I know what you are thinking: "I am not naturally an organized person." Me either. I am horribly disorganized, which drastically increases the importance of having structure.

Set up systems to make being organized comfortable whether you are naturally an organized person or not. Having structure and consistency makes staying focused and organized easier. The more organized operation will almost always rise to the top. Design an office organization that gives clients a good impression and is also efficient.

THOUGHT-PROVOKING QUESTIONS AND ACTION PLANS

1. Will your office location and appearance assist you in attracting the ideal client?

2. Stand outside your office and look at it objectively. What do your prospects and clients see when they drive up to your location? Does your outside appearance impress people or cause them to lose confidence in your business? Explain.

3. Walk through the front door of your business and look around as if you have never been there before. What is your first thought? Does the office look cluttered? Organized? Chaotic? Professional? Tacky? Was your first impression positive or negative? Why?

4. Do you have a place for everything and is everything in its place? Do you have a system for how and where you store items so they can be easily found? If so, what is that system and is everyone on your staff aware of it?

5. What is one specific step you are going to take this week to make your office more aesthetically pleasing and efficient? How are you going to make sure its appearance supports rather than sabotages the perception of professionalism?

6. In what ways do you make it difficult for customers to do business with you? Have you asked them recently?

Micromanage Processes, Don't Micromanage People

*Most people believe that if you go in and try to micromanage
a forest, it is possible to destroy the very thing that makes it
a unique and special place. That's just as true of the Net.*

— GLEN RAPHAEL

I HAVE BEEN ACCUSED of being a micromanager. Micromanaging people
can destroy their uniqueness and stifle creativity. I micromanage processes so that I don't have to micromanage people. In the working world
there are two bosses who will drive you crazy:

- Those who don't give you the time of day
- Those who hover over you while you work

I have worked for both types. I have worked in situations where I
received very little information on what I should be doing. It was frustrat-
ing not to feel comfortable that I was doing a good job.

I have also worked with associates who would ask you to do a job then come back ten minutes later to ask if you had completed the task. Argh!!! Can you imagine how inefficient it is to tell someone to do a task then stand over her to make sure she does it well? Give me a break.

My job is to unleash the growth potential of my employees. People are naturally powerful and successful—remove the barriers in your operation that are keeping them from succeeding and get out of their way. It takes a secure leader to build the skills of others. Empowered employees are more likely to feel a sense of pride and therefore treat the business like it is their own.

It is insulting to have someone hovering overhead. George Patton said, "Don't tell people how to do things. Tell them what to do and let them surprise you with their results." Employees appreciate being treated like intelligent human beings. They will also often come up with a better way if provided the freedom. Once trained they enjoy the challenge of managing themselves.

How do we provide structure and foundation and design systems to assure completion without babysitting employees? Core processes need to be defined. Ideally, the processes are designed simultaneously by employees and leadership.

Here are the steps we went through in setting up clear accountability so we didn't have to micromanage:

- We did personality testing on each individual. Understanding the strengths and weaknesses of each person is paramount.

- We made a list of all processes inside the office (whether done daily, weekly, etc.), such as following up on claims, forwarding the phone at the end of the day, etc.

- Looking at my personality, I determined which jobs allowed me to work within my strengths and generate the most profit for the organization. Those responsibilities became mine and were listed on a sheet. Yes, it may be selfish to say that I get to design my job first, but management needs to build a team that complements the leader. Management's duties should be created by design, not default.

- Looking at the remaining personalities and the remaining jobs, we next decided which three to five of the remaining duties were most crucial. Those jobs were assigned based on personality strengths. The remaining responsibilities were divided up based on the strengths and weaknesses of each person. We each ended up with a fairly equal amount of responsibility (not number of jobs but amount of time required for those jobs).

- The list of job responsibilities exists in a central electronic location to maintain clarity of accountability. Each person has their own list of duties (we call it our goals sheet). Each process is assigned to one person *only*. That guarantees specific accountability. Every person in the operation handles general sales and service.

- The way each job is to be performed is defined in writing. This makes training easy and allows others to take over in the event the primary person responsible for a duty is out temporarily. The electronic document that contains these written processes becomes the operations guide.

- Finally, we created a clear line of sight between the tasks assigned and the company goals. I will be more passionate about calling people who have made a late payment if I understand the effect that will have on client retention. I need to understand the connection between my duties and the organization's objectives. Don't just assign jobs; explain the impact of those processes.

Having clear accountability radically reduces the stress level in the office. There is only one person who could be in trouble if something slips through the cracks. No excuses. Clear expectations. No surprises. Manage processes in a way that allows employees to be self-directed.

THOUGHT-PROVOKING QUESTIONS AND ACTION PLANS

1. Have you ever worked for someone who micromanaged you? What caused the most frustration?

2. Are your business's operational processes defined in writing? If not, will you begin?

3. Is each process inside your business ultimately the responsibility of only one person? Are there checks and balances in place to make sure that the processes are taking place as defined?

4. Do you have more of a tendency to micromanage or provide too little leadership? Once you create a self-sufficient, educated team, do you remember to consistently cheer them on?

Transparently Yours

*To be nobody-but-yourself—in a world which is
doing its best, night and day, to make you everybody
else—means to fight the hardest battle which any
human being can fight and never stop fighting.*

— E. E. CUMMINGS

MS. SOURPUSS'S COMMENT about me being "too professional" crept back into my thoughts for years after the initial event. My pink office was my daily reminder of the encounter. I put a tremendous amount of effort into being an exceptional salesperson, if for no other reason than to prove that I was not "too professional," although I had no idea what too professional meant.

It would be years later that I finally came to a full understanding of how my performance that day was "too professional." I can still recall how much I dreaded being videotaped doing a sales presentation. I prepared like crazy. I walked into the room that morning trying not to recall my fear of being in front of a group. I decided that no one but me was aware that I was uncomfortable. I became determined to fake confidence. I know now that it was my fake confidence that caused my downfall. I was portraying what I perceived to be the perfect salesperson and in doing so, lost myself. My attempt to emulate my perception of the ideal wasn't real. I was not being authentic.

Employees, customers, family, and friends prefer that I am unique, humble, and real. It is very difficult to trust a person who is playing games or spitting out canned scripts.

There have been times when I catch myself trying to be the perfect mother, wife, boss, friend, or salesperson. It is exhausting.

We have the same tendency at work. Who doesn't want to have pride in her ability to do her job? Over the years I have learned to be transparent in every aspect of my life. As e. e. cummings indicated, we must fight to be our authentic selves. The world can be toxic in its attempt to force us to conform to some ideal, but only if we allow ourselves to buy in.

I want customers and employees to understand that I have a real concern for their well-being. I gain joy from seeing them succeed. I no longer expend effort attempting to keep others from seeing who I really am or how I really feel. I fight hard to overcome the urge to be too professional by portraying the consummate salesperson. The mask is gone.

It takes effort to be authentic. It takes even more effort to be inauthentic. Ideally we are each the same person twenty-four hours a day, seven days a week. What I say should match what I do. There should always be congruence between my walk and my talk. I am the same person at work, at home, at church, and at play with friends. There is no compartmentalized life. It is much less exhausting to allow people to see the real me. Customers and employees alike will be much more likely to trust that authenticity.

There are certain times when I am far from perfect but I am committed not to wear a mask. Like it or not, we teach with our lives. If I have a genuine love for people it is obvious. Encourage an authentic organization of transparent people who genuinely care about others.

THOUGHT-PROVOKING QUESTIONS AND ACTION PLANS

1. Have you ever felt the pressure to fake confidence in a situation? Did you wonder whether or not others could see through the act?

2. Do you feel comfortable being completely real with your employees? Are you hesitant to allow them to know when you are struggling? You become more human if you don't pretend to have things under control at all times.

3. Does the message you communicate verbally line up with your life? Do you practice what you preach? Are you leading a life worth emulating? Are you a good role model?

4. Have you noticed how refreshing it is not to pretend to have it all together? Have you discovered that others will be more authentic with you when they are allowed to get to know the real you?

5. Do you ever find yourself spitting out canned scripts to customers or prospects? Are you a transparent person who is able to easily build trust? If you're not sure, ask a friend or employee.

6. Do you have people in your life whom you have figuratively put on a pedestal? Would you have a more authentic relationship with them if you crushed the pretense that they had it all together? Do you allow others to put you on a pedestal by pretending you are self-sufficient and have life under control?

Don't Create Monster Clients

People treat you the way you teach them to treat you.
—JACK CANFIELD

THE FIRST YEAR I opened my agency, I remember feeling desperate to get business. If a prospect was interested, I would drive an hour away to get a signature on an application. I would stay at the office until 10:00 at night to close one more deal. I bent over backward to accommodate clients so they would choose to reward us with their business.

During the second year, I started to grasp how demanding many of my clients had become. Occasionally a client would call and mandate that I drive to their home to pick up a payment. It was not uncommon for a customer to ask me to come to his home to explain a policy.

I realized, albeit a little late, that I had taught my clients to take me for granted and to take advantage of my goodwill. The ones who had unrealistic expectations are the ones whom I had desperately pursued. I had turned them into monsters who expected inappropriate concessions.

I looked in the mirror and asked myself what I wanted our business to stand for. Ann Landers was fond of saying, "If we do not stand for something, we will fall for anything."

Well, I was falling all over myself trying to please clients and it backfired. A customer would not call her accountant or lawyer and demand that he come pick up a payment. It was my fault that I was perceived as unprofessional.

It was time to set boundaries so we would be perceived as professionals instead of doormats. I realized that if I wanted to be deemed as valuable as an attorney or a physician, I needed to start acting like a professional.

We decided to do all applications in the office. We would make exceptions if there were extenuating circumstances that warranted special treatment. Otherwise demanding prospects were referred to other businesses. As you can imagine, the transition was arduous. You may be wondering, "Did you lose some business by being so strict?" Yes we did, but very little. We now had extra time to attract many more customers who were less demanding and more appreciative.

Furthermore, I had more time to focus on the top priorities. I was in the office dealing with clients and prospects face to face, instead of running around the county racking up miles, ratcheting up stress, and wasting valuable time driving to and fro.

And yes, I had to "fire" some of the monster clients who continued to demand special treatment. I blame myself for setting up this unhealthy situation. As diplomatically as I tried to explain the change, a few customers refused to conform. It was clear that continuing to overextend myself would perpetuate their behavior. If they weren't able to treat us like professionals, we were better off to allow them to move on.

Be aware of behaviors that create monster clients. We need to behave in a professional manner to increase the chances that customers will treat us like professionals.

THOUGHT-PROVOKING QUESTIONS AND ACTION PLANS

1. Do you sometimes feel desperate to add new clients? What is something you have done that was above and beyond in order to motivate a prospect to do business with your organization?

2. Does your organization have a proactive communication plan for customers? Do you contact them several times a year using several different approaches? Would your customers say you contact them too much or too little?

3. Do you encourage employees to handle frustrated clients themselves to build the customers' confidence or do staff members transfer all unpleasant calls to you?

4. How has your business created monster customers? How can you avoid them in the future?

5. Do you maintain a pleasant attitude when customers are ridiculous in their demands? Do you bounce back quickly if they frustrate you?

Loving the Difficult

I love complaining customers.
—Peggy Morrow

W E CAN REDUCE the number of monster clients by designing a professional agency and acting like professionals. Most customers are a tremendous pleasure to work with. It is really easy to love customers who come
in with a positive attitude. It is not as easy to love the difficult customers.

There are days when each of us has been the difficult customer. I can
remember occasions when I was impatient with a clerk at the grocery store
or frustrated when fast food was not delivered quickly. We have all been the
customer who has thrown a dirty look or made a sarcastic remark. We have
each also experienced a customer who was clearly having a bad day.

I heard an analogy once that an angry person is like a volcano. When
it is ready to blow you should not try to prevent it. You cannot try to calm
it down. You need to let it blow. Sometimes people get angry because they
feel they are not being heard. They get louder and louder in an effort to force
someone to listen to their point of view.

Customers with legitimate complaints deserve to have someone hear them out. I have found that it is always best to allow them to vent. Once they let the frustration out of their system, they are much more likely to allow me to help them. Now they are ready for resolution.

We try also to remember that often the person who is upset is not really upset with us. Often she has something else going on in her life that is causing the irrational reaction.

There are perpetually unhappy customers. I had a gentleman who was sarcastic and abusive every time he entered our office. The entire staff dreaded his presence. After many inappropriate situations I decided I had had enough. He walked in one day and immediately announced, "I am not happy." I retorted, "You've never been happy once. Why would today be any different? What can I do for you?"

His jaw dropped. He just looked at me. Eventually he said, "I'm not always unhappy."

I lovingly responded, "Yes sir, you are."

That was the last negative incident we ever had with that particular client. Evidently he did not like the way he was perceived. I had figuratively held a mirror up to him and he didn't like the reflection. He still does business with our firm and has never again treated us unkindly or disrespectfully.

Only on rare occasions do we have to be defensive. I would not expect anyone in a business to tolerate cursing or excessive abuse. More often than not, a customer is just having a bad day and needs understanding.

Unfortunately there are occasions when we have to deliver bad news that will cause a negative reaction. We have learned never to postpone bad news. The situation will typically get worse with additional time. The stress will definitely intensify if I postpone that inevitable conversation. If we have bad news to deliver, we stop everything and do it immediately.

Try to prevent customers from becoming angry. Consider it a challenge to turn angry customers into advocates.

THOUGHT-PROVOKING QUESTIONS AND ACTION PLANS

1. Does your business train employees on how to turn difficult customers into advocates for your organization?

2. Do your employees feel comfortable that they have the authority and ability to handle clients who are out of control?

3. Does your organization have a tendency to postpone handling situations that are negative?

4. Do you consider it a challenge to turn complaining customers into allies? Are you good at it?

Don't Let Them Leave Quietly

Your most unhappy customers are your greatest source of learning.
—BILL GATES

I WAS CONTACTING CUSTOMERS who had chosen to sever their relationship with our company. One lady who I called was short in her response. When I asked her why she was no longer going to be doing business with us she replied, "You didn't say hi to me."

I was taken aback. I recalled the last time I had seen this customer. She was making a payment in our reception area. I was running to obtain a file while speaking to another customer on my cordless headset.

I remembered wishing I could stop and say hi. Unfortunately I was on the phone helping someone else. Now she was informing me that she had decided to stop doing business with us because in her mind, I did not value her business.

Have you ever felt that some people will be impossible to please, no matter what you do? That is how I felt that day. I stopped and analyzed the situation. I assumed she would understand because she could clearly hear that my conversation was a business call and see that I was not slacking off. At the time I felt I was doing all I could. I have since decided that it is possible for me to at least acknowledge every customer that I come in contact with, even if it's just a wave.

That call ended with me apologizing. I genuinely felt bad that she felt unappreciated. I did not bother explaining why I had not communicated. The damage had been done and defending myself wouldn't change anything. I was able to make sure the customer understood that I was sorry to lose her. I asked for and obtained permission to contact her in the future to discuss her returning to do business with us.

We contact clients who have chosen to defect to determine ways to improve our operation. Questioning unhappy customers allows us to determine ways we can tweak our operation to improve our service. Throughout daily operations we look for cues that customers are unhappy. We proactively approach customers and ask how the company's services could be improved.

I was working with a new client to design an automobile insurance program. At the end of the process I handed him an identification card and he handed me a check for $600. Half teasingly he waved the card in the air and said, "This is what I get for $600?"

He pretended to be joking but I understood it was really how he felt. He did not think a little piece of paper and a promise was adequate. My office staff and I discussed the situation after he left. We knew if he felt that dissatisfied, he probably wasn't alone. We created a professional welcome kit to provide to new customers. Clearly they wanted to walk away from the process with more than a small piece of paper. We have to listen to customers, then determine whether or not it is appropriate to change operations based on what we've learned.

Regularly communicating with customers reduces defections and increases the likelihood of referrals. We don't just love consumers when we get them. We have to continue to earn their business . . . over and over again.

Don't allow customers to leave quietly. Design processes to open communications. Reduce concerns before the customer leaves. The information gathered from customers should be shared through the organization and operations may change based on this information. Finally, have processes in place to contact defecting customers to see if they will do business with you in the future. Often they realize the grass really isn't greener.

I have been shocked at how often customers are willing to give us a second chance if they see we genuinely care. Interview customers who choose to stop doing business with you to improve operations and attempt to eventually recover them.

THOUGHT-PROVOKING QUESTIONS AND ACTION PLANS

1. Do you have a process in place to determine why customers choose to stop doing business with your firm?

2. Who is the best person in your operation to be making those contacts?

3. Do you regularly look to see if processes in your operation need to be changed based on the feedback received from customers?

4. Does your operation consistently communicate the learning from customer conversations throughout the organization?

5. Is there a process in place to try and recover customers who have chosen to stop doing business with your company?

Don't Do What I Tell You

The spirit, the will to win, and the will to excel are the things that endure. These qualities are so much more important than the events that occur.
—Vince Lombardi

I RECENTLY TOOK A new design to my local printer and asked him to manufacture some business cards. Immediately, Louie began suggesting improvements that could be made on my sketch. Instead of doing what I requested, he gave me what I needed. He was not willing to produce a mediocre product (which was what my idea would have created). It was important to him to add value, to provide his customer with an excellent product. Don't be afraid to recommend what your customer needs.

I would have been pleased if the business cards had been printed as I had originally proposed. My level of satisfaction was drastically increased because he took my idea and improved upon it—without being asked.

So often in the business world, transactions are performed to merely fulfill the customer's request. Yet what we owe the customer is not to do only as asked but to give advice based on our professional expertise. We should have a desire to excel, to go above and beyond.

One size doesn't fit all. We cannot have a cookie-cutter approach to customers. We need to customize presentations based on the needs of each specific customer. We need to answer not only the questions that they ask but also those they don't know to ask.

As a professional, I know where there is most likely to be a possible misunderstanding. I choose to be proactive in educating my prospects and customers. For instance, if a prospective client approaches an insurance agent requesting very specific coverage and the coverage is provided without any discussion, that agent is performing a horrible disservice. Do not just fill orders, ask questions!

My favorite question is "What formula did you use to determine the amount of liability coverage you currently carry was right for you?" The response, literally 100 percent of the time, is a blank stare. If I pause appropriately, allowing the magnitude of the situation to penetrate the client's mind, the panic look starts to kick in.

Being in business is not about giving a customer what he or she asks for but imparting to him or her the essential information pertaining to actual needs. The decisions belong to the customer, once I have given him the appropriate education. He lives with the consequences.

Occasionally I will encounter a prospect or client who does not want to explore her actual needs. My comment is always "I have been involved in many situations where a client found out exactly what was and was not covered only at the time of a claim. Let's take a few minutes now so that we reduce the chances that you'll have a surprise at claim time."

I inherited a customer many years ago. For three years in a row I literally begged this gentleman to allow me to review coverage with him. His response was always "I know what I have. I do not need to review my coverage." Each time I would remind him that we needed to verify that he had appropriate limits, understood sufficiently what was covered, and was obtaining all of the discounts he was eligible for.

One day the customer called screaming. There had been a fire at one of his homes and he didn't have enough coverage. He was furious with me because the amount of money he would receive was going to be $25,000 less than what it would take to rebuild the house.

I gently reminded him that I had tried several times in the last three years to review coverage with him. Emotion trumped reason and logic fell on deaf ears. My customer continued to scream and eventually hung up on me.

Twenty minutes later, he called back and apologized. "I know you are right. It is my fault that I am underinsured. You tried to do your job. I am sorry I was rude. I am not angry with you, I am frustrated with myself." I knew I had done everything in my power but felt no satisfaction when he was not appropriately covered.

I use this example frequently when people inform me that they do not care about reviewing their insurance. I do not want the satisfaction of being right if a customer does not have the appropriate coverage. I want the satisfaction of knowing my customers will have what they need in the event of a claim.

Give your clients the advice that you would want someone to give to you. Be willing to walk away from a potential customer if you are unable to offer a product that appropriately meets his or her needs.

Know the competition well enough to know where to send customers you are unable to help. Have a will to excel. I am not willing to just do my job. It is crucial that I am doing it to the best of my ability. As a true professional I will feel a sense of responsibility to excel by offering clients what is in their best interest.

THOUGHT-PROVOKING QUESTIONS AND ACTION PLANS

1. Have you created an atmosphere where employees proactively look for ways to go above and beyond customers' expectations?

2. Does your team meet on a regular basis and discuss ways that they can provide service that will add value?

3. Does your business consistently ask customers what could be done to improve the level of service?

4. Do you understand what types of issues cause your customers stress? How can you provide solutions to situations that may be keeping them up at night?

Take Your Own Advice

A word to the wise isn't necessary—
it's the stupid ones that need the advice.
— BILL COSBY

A S PROFESSIONALS WE work hard to provide customers with sound advice. It is important that we stay well educated so we are able to customize programs for customers based on their specific needs. We need to have a system in place to make sure we look at each customer's individual situation to determine how we can best provide for his needs.

Stop and think about whether or not you are currently taking your own advice. If you were to customize a program for yourself based on the process you typically use with customers—would you take your own advice?

Think about the advice that you give your customers during the day. Are you doing things in a manner that is consistent with the advice you typically bestow? It is hard to believe but people who dispense advice all day long at times do not heed their own recommendations.

Have you ever known a plumber with a leaky faucet? Have you ever known a physician who was so overweight that you questioned his credibility as he gave you advice regarding your health?

There are insurance agency owners who do not protect their assets in a manner consistent with what they would recommend to their clients. There are financial planners who have not begun contributing to their own retirement program. Scary but true.

Stop and look at what you do. If your clients could see the way you handle your personal decisions, would they have faith in your ability to advise them? It is very difficult to sell a product that you do not believe in. If I am not confident enough in the product that I would buy it myself, chances are that the prospective customer will see right through me.

It is not uncommon for me to be very specific with customers about exactly what products I personally have purchased. When I make this disclosure I typically see that the customer is much more comfortable with the purchase of a product.

Many were following their own advice at one time but quit. Conditions change and we do not always do a good job of reevaluating our own personal situation. I need to look at my affairs and determine what advice I would provide myself, then follow it. To have credibility in my industry and with customers I need to determine whether or not I am personally following the advice that I give others.

THOUGHT-PROVOKING QUESTIONS AND ACTION PLANS

1. If your customers considered your personal situation, would they be shocked that you do not take the advice you give them?

2. Do those who work with you believe in your product and follow the advice that they would provide your customers? Why or why not?

3. What one thing that relates to your business would you advise yourself to do differently?

4. Was there a time when you were following the advice you would have provided but quit? Why did you quit?

Don't Go Back Like a Tornado

Change is the end result of all true learning. Change involves three things: First, a dissatisfaction with self—a felt void or need; second, a decision to change—to fill the void or need; and third, a conscious dedication to the process of growth and change—the willful act of making the change: Doing Something.
— DR. FELICE LEONARDO BUSCAGLIA

WE HAVE TO be willing to reinvent our businesses often or run the risk of becoming obscure. Some people love this, some hate it. I did a series of speaking engagements in Seattle, Washington. On my third trip a business owner said, "My employees hate it when you come to town. After you leave, I go back so excited that I tear up the office like a tornado."

I could not help but laugh, but I was horrified at the same time. Have you ever left a presentation with a huge list of things you are going to implement? Most people become overwhelmed or just forget the potential change once they get back into the "real" world.

Two negative things could occur after you go to a great presentation or read a book that provides insight:

- You could go back and do too much. Implementing radical changes too quickly can intimidate employees.
- You could go back and do nothing. The additional knowledge is irrelevant if it is not executed.

Transformation is not optional. Businesses are works in progress— we will never be "finished." We need to adapt to market and technology advances and consumer preferences.

Change should be implemented slowly and intentionally with clear communications along the way. The level of change that will take place in your world will be one of the determinants of your success. How do you implement changes without causing chaos?

There is a right way and a wrong way to make changes.

- Sit down with core leadership and create a clear vision of the overall changes that need to be made. If multiple changes are needed, make a list of all of the changes and prioritize them. Get up in the helicopter and consider how changes in one area of the organization may affect other parts of the organization.
- Create a clear strategy and specific action plan to implement changes. Contemplate what personnel and resources will be necessary for execution of the plan.
- Communicate the vision to those throughout the organization. There needs to be a clear understanding of not only what changes are to be made but also how those changes will affect all parties involved. The communication should articulate why changes are needed to create a sense of urgency throughout the organization.
- Empower the team to execute the changes. Provide training as you redesign operations. Provide feedback regarding the progress of changes while celebrating small wins. Continue to improve by paying attention to the details and getting feedback from all of the parties involved.

- Limit the number of changes that will happen simultaneously. The chances of success and the ability to measure that success are drastically reduced if you are trying to make too many changes at once.

I have found that craving change is a key to success. Yes, I realize I have said this more than once. Many businesses become crippled and frustrated when change is mandated. The feeling of lack of control causes some to complain and become nonfunctional.

Success in life is increased drastically if you thrive on change. Start by coming to the realization that you and your operation are not perfect. Once you have created a plan, operate with the clear understanding and acceptance that life will force you to be able to adapt at times. Implement changes in a strategic manner that inspires the team.

THOUGHT-PROVOKING QUESTIONS AND ACTION PLANS

1. Do you thrive on change or would you prefer to maintain the status quo?

2. How do your employees react when they realize change is inevitable? Do they support change or fight it?

3. What obstacles have you run into when trying to implement change? What do you think could have been done to improve the change process?

4. Do you implement changes slowly enough that others are not overwhelmed? Are you willing to be unwavering in resolution when you have to deal with an employee who resists change?

5. Are you determined to ensure that changes are implemented when needed?

Odds Are, I Caused It

*Level 5 leaders look out the window to apportion credit
to factors outside themselves when things go well. They
look in the mirror to apportion responsibility.*
—JIM COLLINS

I RECEIVED A PHONE call this week from a business owner. The call began
with "I lost three employees this week, and I need you to help me find
three new people . . . quick." My first reaction was to give him information
on how to search for the next employee. Then I stopped. Wait a minute, I
contemplated, why did he lose three employees?

A business that is running on all cylinders has a clear vision, empowered
employees, and strong systems. The business is successful because it is on
autopilot, not because of a specific leader. The system works with or without
the boss because the people want to do a good job. Employees work hard
whether the leader is present or not. They work hard because they have clear
direction, trust the leadership, and know that the leadership genuinely cares
about employees and customers.

When some portion of the business isn't working well, it's only natural to treat the symptoms. In this case, we could put a Band-Aid on a situation that clearly needs major surgery. We could easily throw three new employees into the office but obviously there is a problem that needs to be dealt with.

The business owner did not need three new employees as badly as he needed to determine what was causing employees to leave. If we did not tackle the situation that caused the employees to leave in the first place, he would probably be dealing with massive turnover again soon.

I love Jim Collins's perspective. Business owners need to point to the team when things are going well. Give the team kudos when they are pulling together and the business is successful.

I learned a long time ago that when things are not going well, odds are I caused the problem! When things aren't working, don't point a finger—look in the mirror.

The process to determine what was causing this specific issue needed to include a detailed exit interview with the three employees when they left. Hopefully the business owner would be able to have frank conversations with each to see how the situation could have been avoided. In addition, this would be a wonderful time to have private conversations with the other employees working in the same department. Maybe they would be able to provide insight as to the issue that was causing dissatisfaction.

When things go wrong in your business, you can go through the fundamentals of business to determine changes that may be needed. In this situation the mental process may be as follows:

Autopilot Leadership

Am I being the leader needed to attract and retain the best employees? Is the business under control and are tasks delegated in an appropriate manner? Am I showing the correct balance of leadership and management skills in my interaction with personnel? Are my actions consistently helping the team toward a clear goal?

Upfront Alignment

Does the correct foundation exist? Do I have a strong business plan and marketing plan in place? Do the employees have a handbook that sets clear expectations for staff members? Does the business have clear, written goals that inspire employees? Is the compensation plan aligned with company goals and competitive for my area?

Team on Target

Are we sure that we attract employees who have the skills necessary to do the job? Do the employees have a clear line of sight between the company goals and the jobs they perform? Is education valued within the organization? Does management provide feedback in a manner that allows two-way communication? Do team members work well together?

Devil's in the Details

Do employees feel prepared to handle daily responsibilities? Are tasks clearly defined in writing? Do employees feel confident that they have the ability to locate necessary information to do their jobs? Do we communicate well with our customers? Do we transfer confidence throughout the organization?

When a problem arises within a business, the manager needs to do a gut check. Instead of running to treat the symptom, we need to look for the actual cause of the problem.

Typically warning signs alert us when something is not ideal in the business. We need to be willing to proactively tackle the issues although it may be easier to attempt to work around them by ignoring them.

The next time there is an issue inside of the business, look in the mirror. Humbly admit, odds are you caused it!

THOUGHT-PROVOKING QUESTIONS AND ACTION PLANS

1. Have you ever had a gut feeling that something was not working well within the business? Did you proactively tackle the issue? Why or why not?

2. Do you have a business partner or mentor you can talk to when you are struggling with some aspect of your business?

3. Is your natural tendency to blame staff members when some portion of the business is not operating well?

4. Are you able to humbly admit to the team when you have done something that caused the business not to operate well? Do you allow yourself to be vulnerable and work with the team to design a better system?

EPILOGUE

I HOPE THIS BOOK has inspired you to begin running your business in a manner that is consistent with an organization that will become a multimillion-dollar corporation. Start designing a business today where you are able to strategically relinquish control. More important, implement the strategies that will allow you to manage your life and enjoy your job.

I hope you feel prepared to design a business that works without you, not because of you. Ideally you will build a company full of employees who think and act like owners.

Ultimately the result of this process is the development of a company that allows the owners and employees to enjoy their role in the business while staying focused on building a truly balanced life.